Press 1 and Pray

And Other Letters from Voice Jail

❖

JOSH FREED

Véhicule Press

Véhicule Press gratefully acknowledges the on-going support of
The Canada Council for the Arts for its publishing program.

Cover design: J. W. Stewart
Cover photo: Thomas Leon Königsthal, Jr.
Cover imaging: André Jacob
Special assistance: Vicki Marcok, Anne Dardick
Typeset in Bembo by Simon Garamond
Printing: AGMV-Marquis Inc.

03 02 01 00   4 3 2 1

CANADIAN CATALOGUING IN PUBLICATION

Freed, Josh, 1949-
Press 1 and Pray : and other letters from voice jail

ISBN 1-55065-143-9

I. Canadian wit and humor (English)
I. Title. II. Title: Press one and pray

PN6178.C3F742 2000   C818'.5402   C00-901148-X

Véhicule Press
www.vehiculepress.com

Distributed by General Distribution Services.

Printed in Canada.

For Ingrid, Daniel, Mike, and Mum

Contents

Introduction

In my last book a few years ago, I included a trilogy of tales called "The Gull War," detailing my battle with a ferocious flock of pigeons (led by Attila the Hen) that had taken control of my balcony. Since then, I've received an onslaught of calls from readers seeking advice on their own pigeon problems.

Should they poison their birds or pet them, scare them off with fake owls or buy a cat? Should they shroud their balconies in pigeon netting, or just plant some land mines? And by the way, do I make house calls?

Having spent hundreds of hours dispensing information on the subject, I've decided it would be unwise to include any pigeon tales in this volume. Mention is made of chickens, beavers, pigs, hummingbirds, cougars, cod and polar bears. I also deal with the sinking Canadian loony and the galloping American buck — but I am obliged to warn that there are no pigeons whatsoever to be found in this book, or on my balcony, which is how I like it.

In the absence of pigeons, I've found no shortage of other dilemmas to tackle, including many important subjects of our time: tight neckties, whining and dining, ice storm survivor guilt, light-fingered bicycle thieves, lead-footed language police and cross-border shopping for "gas and a bypass."

Several stories touch on interactive phone technology, the new push-button answering systems that make our lives better and worse at the same time. This technology reflects a larger world of endless small choices, where you rarely find the choice you want. There just aren't enough buttons to push, whether you're shopping for a mattress, a name for your child or a new country in a referendum.

As a rule, the more important the decision the fewer options you're offered, which is why America has 70 types of conditioning shampoo and only three candidates for president; and why Quebec's referendum question offered only a YES or a NO — with no room for any maybes.

In most cases, the best you can do is select the option that seems least confusing, and pray you've made the right choice; then, when it turns out you're wrong, try to keep some perspective. Things usually look better later, if you can last until then, and it helps to stay in good humour.

For he who laughs, lasts.

That's why I write my column in the Montreal *Gazette* every Saturday, at the end of my week, when annoying experiences often start to seem amusing. It's my chance for perspective every week, and this book represents my perspective over the last five years.

Many of the stories take place in Montreal, where nothing ever works like it's supposed to, but everything somehow works fine. Other stories take place as far away as Hong Kong and Syria, because life's small problems follow you everywhere and the best revenge is writing.

If I didn't write a column I'd probably be in therapy, paying someone to listen to my stories instead of getting paid for telling them. So I hope you enjoy reading these tales as much as I've enjoyed writing them. And I'm sorry if you have a pigeon problem and bought the wrong book.

Because, no, I don't make house calls.

Thanks to the many people who in some way help to create my weekly world: my wife Ingrid, always my first reader and critic; Stephen Phizicky whose Friday calls make Saturday columns more fun; also to Victor Dabby, Jon Kalina, Tom Puchniak, and Janet Torge who are always there to lend an earful.

At the Montreal *Gazette*, thanks to Catherine Sedgwick, and the other patient souls at the desk who know too well that I'm a charter member of life's last minute club. More thanks to Simon Dardick my editor at Véhicule Press, one of the rare text doctors who still makes house calls.

ONE

Breaking Out of E-Jail

UNROMANCING THE PHONE

❖

WELCOME! — to our automated page 3 column.

All our writers are currently occupied. Please stay on the page to retain your reading priority. If you know what kind of column you wish to read, you can save time by making the following selection.

- To read about chickens, PRESS 1 and wait for page 127.
- For a Dave Barry column, PRESS 2 and wait till tomorrow.
- If you'll read anything, PRESS ON.

Beep.

I was in a phone booth recently, trying to get a number from 411, but as usual there was no operator, just a machine interrogating me with slow, boring questions: Did I want French or English? Business or residence? For what city ... what street...what cellblock?

I replied in one-word monotones until it asked what name I wanted. "Groevik," I said, then blurted: "It's Norwegian, so I'm not sure if it's spelled o-e or e-o. Oh, I just remembered it's actually spel —"

"Please wait," broke in the machine, cutting me off in mid-sentence. Then it left me hanging in cyberphonespace for more than a minute, while an operator presumably looked up a variety of wrong spellings.

"Hello," I shouted into the phone, "Hell-o-oo!"

"Please wait," repeated the machine, every ten seconds, until finally, I lost my temper and bellowed. "Would someone take the damn phone!...I hate this system!"

I heard a click, and a wounded female voice.

"Sir ... why are you are being aggressive to me? You don't have the right to treat me that way."

I tried to explain to the woman that I was angry at the machine — not her — but it was too late. Technology had ruined another relationship.

Frankly, I've been getting cranky with more and more service people on the phone lately when I'm really mad at their machines. Every time I dial a bank, train or government number, I spend five minutes pushing buttons like a rat in a maze. Even the smallest companies seem to be part of it.

"Welcome to Ralph's Toaster Repair Shop. For pop-up toasters, press 1. For manual toasters, press 2. For thick-slice baguette and bagel toasters, press 3. For extra-large rye toasters, Arabic pita toasters, Belgian croissant warmers ..."

Press one option and five new choices greet you. By the time you've listened to all of them, you're so confused you've forgotten why you called in the first place. Airlines and trains are the worst, because you know some people are getting out of the maze faster than you.

Beep.

Thanks for calling "No-People Airlines." All our operators have been fired. Please stay on the line and prepare to be humiliated by computer. Members of our Prestige and Elite clubs may press O to speak to a service representative now. Economy travellers, listen carefully:

Beep.

● For flight information about northeastern routes, Tuesday and Saturday, May 13 through July 7, PRESS 1.
● For advance booking for three or more people, weekdays, from noon to 4 p.m. and 6 to 9 a.m., excluding Wednesdays, PRESS 2.
● To speak to an agent, prepare three days of food and water by your phone, and please hold. We *value* your business."

By the time you get the airline's one overworked employee on the line, you're ready to strangle him and he hasn't even opened his mouth. Part of the problem is that the early generations of phone machines are under-qualified for the job. In an era when IBM's "Deep Blue" computer can outthink the world's smartest chess player, our phone machine computers can't think 1/10th as fast as Mable the Operator.
As customers, we are stuck with "Superficial Blue."

Consider those automated company phone directories where you have to punch the letters of the employee you want into your phone. If you're like me, you're never quite sure how to spell anyone's name. Is it Beetman? Or Beitmann? Or Bietman?

If you were talking to Mable, she'd just say "Oh you mean Mr.

Boethamien, the nice man who works in billing."

But a machine doesn't make that leap. It doesn't think in shades of gray, only in boring black or white, and it forces us to think that way too.

The real problem is that the machines must deal with human beings — a complex, contradictory lot who often don't know what we want. We don't want to make a train reservation for 1) Tuesday or 2) Wednesday. We want to know what it costs first, and if there are any seat sales. Or is it cheaper to go on weekends?

If IBM wants to do humanity a favor, it should forget about building a machine to outthink humans and create one to think like a human; a machine that would adapt to our indecision rather than forcing us to keep making decisions.

Until then, there's only one way for us humans to fight back against the (phone) system. Let's go on strike. Next time you call a bank, airline or 411, refuse to play by their rules and press zero for an operator.

If we all press zero all the time, maybe the people behind the machines will figure out what we think of their system. Support the human race.

Press zero now.

GET LOST

❖

THEY'RE PUTTING a fancy new gadget in luxury cars these days to make sure you never get lost: It's a Global Positioning System (GPS) that plots your location by satellite and guides you right to your destination.

Some might cheer this as progress, but I think it's just one more way to take the excitement out of life. I've just returned from a trip to Europe and North Africa, where some of my most fascinating experiences took place when I was lost. You learn a lot about a place when you don't know where you are.

We started our trip in southern Tunisia, where a wrong turn can land you in the Sahara Desert. Tunisians are always happy to give directions but they're tricky to understand, because many people consider it rude to point with your finger.

Ask someone for the nearest hotel, and they'll wave their hand in a polite little circle that points everywhere at once. The trick, I discovered, is to watch people's noses, because that's how they indicate directions. Typical was a gentleman in a long robe we stopped for advice, at a three-way intersection en route to the desert town of Douz.

"Turn there," he said in broken French, nodding his nose delicately toward the sand dunes. I couldn't tell whether he meant the road south, or a diagonal road to the southwest.

"Do you mean that road there?" I said, pointing my arm rudely. "Or ... *that* one?"

"There!" he said, nodding his nose imperceptibly again. I still didn't understand, and we both grew exasperated. I wanted to shout, "Could you just point the right way!" while he wanted to shout, "Ignoramus! It's as plain as the nose on my face!"

After our lengthy conversation was over, I thanked him and followed his directions. Not surprisingly, I took the wrong road and had to ask more people for directions, but it only made the trip more interesting.

Now compare this process with travelling in Sicily, just north of Tunisia, where we also spent a week driving by car. Sicilians are an expressive people who talk with their hands, using each finger as if it were a verb. Stop someone for directions, and they'll lean into your car and start waving their hands about, visually conjuring up each traffic light and overpass in their instructions.

One police officer leaned so far into the driver's window he was practically in the passenger seat as he gave me passionate non-stop directions in Italian for almost five minutes. I have no idea what he said but, judging from his hands, I think it sounded something like this:

First you go north three blocks until you pass a little trattoria — they make a wonderful Fettuccini Norma with lots of garlic, if you have time to eat. Then, go left until you pass La Casa de Napoli — I recommend the proscuitto — it's wonderful! Then, you take a sharp right and pass the cemetery...you know, that was where I kissed my first woman twenty-one years ago!

"God, she was beautiful — a madonna! — but she married a building contractor. What a waste!...Anyway, you turn right at Albini's cheese shop — try the parmesan — and two stores later, you are there!

After their performance is over, most Sicilians will insist on taking you halfway there anyway, jumping onto their motor scooters and driving two kilometres out of their way, then stopping to give you five more minutes of instructions before they leave. The last you see of them as they disappear into the distance is their hand waving a lavish goodbye.

Our last experience was in England, where directions are fairly straight-forward, except for the fact the British speak a strange English dialect that in no way resembles normal North American English.

Well, lovey, you just follow the motorway straight on until it becomes dual carriageway, then you go over the Hammersmith flyover, past the roundabout and continue on till you pass the second layby.

Still with me? Good. Take a sharp right at the first four-way — mind the coppers as you do or they'll nick you — then slow down and you'll pass the lorry shop and two more four-ways. Turn right at Pete's chip stand and carry on past the T-junction by the next flyover, where you hang a right and, well, Bob's your uncle.

All of which is to say the most entertaining part of driving a car is getting lost and the last thing we need is some new-fangled gadgetry that allows us to find our way around without talking to anyone. In fact, I have only one thing to say to the designers of this new space-age technology: Get lost.

ELECTRONIC HIGHWAY ROBBERY

❖

Last year, I signed up with Unitel, a new Canadian phone company that promises big long-distance savings. But when this month's bill arrived, I wasn't thrilled with the discount. I'd made about $10 worth of calls — and my bill was $846.57.

I could hear the ad slogan: "UNITEL! Only 8,460 per cent more than your regular long-distance company!"

My bill included calls to Turkey, Germany, Portugal, Switzerland and the "Indian Republic," countries where I don't know a soul. Someone else was obviously using my phone line, but who? It was the start of a technological mystery, with me playing cyberspace Sherlock. According to the bill, all the calls were made from inside my home, not on a credit card. I mentally ran through a list of recent houseguests: Had anyone spent a long time in the den?

I also considered the possibility of a burglar, but nothing in the house was missing. Could someone have broken in just to use the phone — was I the victim of a long-distance phone-call thief?

Several of the calls were made to Brampton, Ont., and Brooklyn, N.Y. I called the New York number to see who lived there and a man answered.

"Hi," I said. "I was just wondering . . . uh . . . who are you?"

"Who are you?" he answered suspiciously.

I explained my problem and he said he was a student from Barbados, studying in New York. I didn't know him and he didn't want to talk to me.

In Brampton, I talked to Amin, who said he was from Ghana. I didn't know him either, but he was sympathetic about my bill.

"You owe $800!?" he said. "Man, if I were you I'd deal with this problem now before things get out of hand."

I took his advice and called the 800-number for Unitel where I wound up talking to Trish, an operator in Winnipeg. She asked me the usual security questions and we went over my bill. Then she spotted something bizarre: all the calls had been made the same night, at the same time, on the same phone line.

I had made a one-hour call to Belgium at 5:47 p.m. Then at 5:51 p.m., only 4 minutes later, I had made a simultaneous three-hour call to Switzerland. Soon after, I had made a two-hour call to Turkey, while I was still talking to Switzerland and Belgium!

I was the victim of a telephone poltergeist that could make several international calls at once. What was going on?

Trish said she'd talk to "security." An hour later, she called back to say they had solved the mystery. A computer "hacker" had broken into the system and stolen my "access" number, she explained. Then the hacker had apparently sold my number to other people who had all used it the same night, before security could trace them. It was electronic highway robbery.

According to Trish, Unitel's security had spotted the problem within hours of the calls and had cancelled my access number (though not my bill). But the damage was done. Someone had run a kind of fly-by-night discount phone-call company for phone thieves, offering special discount rates on my line!

Trish said to forget the bill, so I can't be too angry at Unitel, which reacted quickly and politely. But the experience has made me a more suspicious citizen of the global electronic village. Nowadays, it's not enough to bolt your windows, bar the door and install a car alarm.

You have to worry about invisible thieves: computer hackers and phone-line hijackers who hang around dark corners in cyberspace. They steal your money and you don't even know it's gone. Like many people, I don't know the information highway from the Laurentian Autoroute — and now I don't trust it either. If someone can steal my phone line, what else do I have to keep an eye on?

Will they steal my pay-TV cable signal and bill me for 5,000 screenings of "Dumb and Dumber," watched everywhere from Moncton to Medicine Hat? Is someone reading this story as I write it and preparing to publish it before me?

Can Finance Minister Paul Martin pull a fast one and slip the federal debt onto my Visa bill?

Total July bill: $42 billion.

As we line up to enter a brave new electronic world, I wonder what new electronic scams lie ahead. For instance, the government wants to give us new Medicare cards with a microchip that contains our entire medical history, but I worry that a hacker will stick me with the bill for a liver transplant in Florida.

There is growing excitement about home shopping, electronic voters' lists and living-room elections where you vote on your TV screen. No thanks. I think I'll do my shopping and voting the old-fashioned way — by foot. Travelling on the information highway is still a bit tricky. Just because you still have your wallet, doesn't mean someone hasn't picked your pocket.

YES, WE HAVE NO MUSHRATOS

❖

I WANDERED INTO MY SUPERMARKET the other day and to my surprise, the tomatoes were gone. According to a sign on the bin, they had been merged with the mushrooms to create a new vegetable called a "mushrato."

A spokesman for mushroom growers had reportedly issued a statement saying: "This gives us a chance to diversify, broaden our market share and expand into new vegetable markets! It's a win-win situation for mushrooms and tomatoes. However, we regret to announce that 25,000 fungi will be laid off."

★ ★ ★

If it hasn't happened yet, it can't be far off. In recent months there have been more merger announcements in the papers than marriages. Film companies, phone companies, oil companies, record companies and movie-record-whiskey companies; everyone's tying the corporate knot in the new Merger-of-the-Week.

If the trend continues, there won't be any single companies left. No wonder our banks keep trying to get hitched; who wants to be a bachelor bank, when you barely get to fondle any assets?

The new business mantra is "bigger or bankrupt." In fact, I keep expecting to get a letter saying:

"Dear Mr. Freed, We regret to inform you that your family has been merged with the Smiths at 4030 St. Urbain St. From now on, you will be known as the Friths."

With the marriage rate tumbling, perhaps newpapers should replace their Births, Marriages and Obituaries section with a Mergers and Downsizing page: "H. Ford and G. Motors tied the knot today in a lavish $6-billion ceremony, celebrated by declaring 30,000 workers redundant."

"Disney Company has announced that the Canadian Mounties would be downsized from a police force to a cartoon."

We're told that merger fever is about synergy and expanding market possibilities. That's why Loblaw's is opening a bank inside its supermarkets, while the banks want to sell insurance and lease cars. In fact, if the banks have their way, they'll soon do everything but your banking — they're getting way too big for that.

And what new "synergetic" partnerships will we see next? Will Kleenex Co. merge with Garden Cemetery Funeral Homes? Will the Roman Catholic church link up with Quebec casinos to provide one-stop Sin-and-Confession?

Can it be long before St. Joseph's Oratory unites with the Spanish and Portuguese Synagogue to create Uni-Temple, featuring baptisms in front and brisses in back? Or until the Expos and the Canadiens merge into the CanExpos, with a goalie who doubles as a catcher?

Not only companies are merging. Toronto merged several munici-palities to form a megacity, and there are rumours it now wants to absorb Hamilton, Buffalo and Halifax. Montreal is also planning a megacity, and some favour merging with Toronto.

This would combine Toronto's clean streets and good libraries with Montreal's cheap housing and nearby Laurentian cottages. On the down-side, we'd spend a lot more time in traffic every morning, commuting from Snowdon to Scarborough.

Elsewhere, Europe's currencies have merged into the Euro, and to keep up, Canada may have to merge its 66-cent dollar with Australia's 57-cent dollar to create one U.S. dollar.

Mergers even dominate politics these days, where one-stop shopping is now the hottest vote in town. To listen to some party leaders, there's no such thing as left or right, liberal or conservative any more. That's why Bill Clinton is the first Democrat to lead a Republican Party and Liberal Jean Chrétien now leads a Conservative one. Tony Blair has successfully crossed the Tories with British Labour, and here in Quebec, the PQ and the Liberals have merged ideas too. Their parties have different names and different positions on sovereignty, but on other policies they parrot each other so closely they could save money and print the same platform.

No industry is changing faster than my own, Canadian newspapers, where there have been so many mergers we are quickly becoming Unipaper. First, Conrad Black traded four papers for the *Financial Post* and future considerations, said to include Michael Jordan. Then the *National Post* bought the *Financial Post*, and half the other papers in the country; then a TV company bought the *National Post* and anything else it could swallow.

Syndicated writers are spreading, and independent views may soon disappear into one large emerging black hole. Frankly, as a dissenting voice in this, it seems to me that we are being con...

We are sorry to interrupt this column, but due to our new format all columns must be the same size and opinion in order to help us perform more efficiently for you. To enhance this restructuring, Mr. Freed's opinion has been merged with several others. Please look in on this new feature next week when "Unicolumn" debuts.

It will appear on Page E6, beside the advertisements for mushratos.

DAYLIGHT CRAVING TIME

❖

Hey buddy, can you spare some time?

DON'T BE SURPRISED if a panhandler asks you that question soon, because time is changing fast. It is now the most badly-needed commodity around, far more valuable than money. According to a recent study by the Heart and Stroke Foundation, 43% of Canadians feel stressed and overwhelmed by lack of time (the other 57% didn't have time to fill out the survey).

"There simply aren't enough hours in the day for most Canadians to accomplish all they want or need to do," said a psychiatrist involved in the study, most likely just before she rushed out the door to pick up the kids.

Welcome to modern time. A mere millennium ago, the 24-hour day was more than enough to spend a hard day in the fields, with plenty of time left over to sit in the dark until you fell asleep from boredom. But nowadays, 24 hours just doesn't suit our schedules.

We have places to phone, things to download and people to e-mail. We must juggle three jobs, two families and four sports. The more succesful we are, the less time we have. The machine age was supposed to free us up for more leisure time, but instead we work harder to keep up with machines. A second saved is rarely a second earned.

Even longtime laggards are speeding up. Spain is cancelling its traditional noontime nap to keep up with Europe's pace, and France is ending its long lunch. Time is becoming a bigger source of tension than money.

Saskatchewan farmers voted not to adapt Daylight Savings Time again, so they'll have more light at the end of the day. But they face opposition from Saskatchewan city folk who want more light in the morning, when they lug their kids to school. There just isn't enough light to go around anymore.

Despite 24-hour convenience stores, movies and hair salons there simply aren't enough hours in a day. We need a solution to all the stress, and there's no time to spare, let me offer a couple of quick proposals. It's time for the incredible, expanding:

■ 25-HOUR DAY. This idea came to me last October 31st, as I raced around in my usual panic trying to cram too many things into too little time. Suddenly I realized it was the day the clocks change and I'd forgotten to turn my watch backward. In seconds, I had gained an hour — and that extra hour made my day just right. I finished everything I had to do and had time leftover to plan the next day.

Why not add an hour to every day? If we can't squeeze our lives into the time available, let's lengthen time to fit our lives. A 25-hour day would be a good start.

Think of it — you'd have an extra hour every day to see the kids, read a book, shop, or channel-flick. Overall, you'd gain one hour a day for 365 days a year — a total of 365 hours — or about fifteen days. You could save it all up and take a holiday!

Ridiculous, you say? A 24-hour day is as natural as the earth turning on its axis, isn't it? Not at all. Modern sleep research shows that when human beings are left alone for several days, in a dark room without clocks, we start to rely on our own inner body clock. And that internal clock works on a 25-hour cycle.

Our natural biological rhythm is actually set for about 25 hours a day, which is probably why so many people have sleep problems — as our poor 25-hour bodies rush to keep up with earth's frenetic 24-hour daily clock. No wonder we're stressed out.

It's time that time stopped for us, I say. The only downside of my system is that each day we'd fall another hour behind the 24-hour sun— until eventually we'd be going to work in the dark. Big deal! We Canadians already spend half our day in the dark during winter, working in artificial light. What's the difference if we spend the rest of our day in the dark too?

■ 28-HOUR DAY. This is a brilliant idea I stumbled on while browsing the internet to research my 25-hour day theory. To my surprise, I discovered a group arguing for an even longer day.

Under this system we would have a six-day week of 28 hours a day. (This adds up to 168 hours, exactly the same as a 24-hour, seven-day week.) They call their plan "a new clock for a new age"— and it makes great sense.

The 28-hour day would let us work ten hours a day, and still have eight hours left over to spend on fun, as well as ten additional extra hours remaining for a good night's sleep. There would be more time for everything: we'd sleep longer, work longer and spend more time with

our family. Best of all, we'd only work four (ten-hour) days a week —
then enjoy two long 28-hour days on the weekend.

The plan's authors call it "the amazing sun-drenched 56-hour weekend."

Critics might argue that the whole system is out of whack with the
sun, because every day would have different hours of light and dark than
the one before. It runs completely contrary to nature. But the plan's
inventors claim this is actually an *advantage*.

Every day of the week would have a different character, they say.
"One day you might have lunch under the stars. Another day you might
breakfast at sunset." It would make the days more memorable than the
identical drab days we have now. To boot, we'd never have the Monday
blahs again, because in their six-day-a-week system, they'd simply cancel
Monday.

Why let ourselves be tyrannized by time? It's time we tyrannized
time. And if you don't like my suggestions, you can devise your own
systems to suit you. Some people might prefer to have a 21-hour, eight-
day week. Others might like a 42-hour, four-day week. Different age
groups might like their own time zones too. For instance, teenagers
often like to sleep till noon, and might come up with their own system
for reducing stress, like only being awake when their parents are asleep.

Of course, there is one last idea that might reduce stress. We could
all just work less, juggle fewer things and slow down, but that's not very
realistic nowadays. Besides, who's got time to think about it when we're
all so tired and stressed out there's no time to think about *anything*. I
mean that's the problem, isn't it?

Gotta run.

CLUB CLUB

❖

I WAS BUYING some fax paper recently when the cashier asked if I wanted to join the store's "office supply club."

No, I explained. I was already a member of two other office supply clubs.

"OK," shrugged the woman. "Then you'll have to pay 20% more for your fax paper. Club members get a special discount."

Minutes later, I was filling out a two-page form, and soon I had a brand-new card to add to my card-stuffed wallet. Club membership used to get you oak-panelled rooms, crystal decanters and $50 cigars, but all my cards get me is discount tires and a few free tows.

I belong to the Canadian Tire Club and the Canadian Automoble Club. I have cards from five video clubs, four frequent flyer plans, three frequent phone call clubs and a discount coffee club, (buy four pounds, get a half pound free).

My "discount steerburger card" gets me an extra cheeseburger for every seventh one I eat; my special "ice cream card" gives me every tenth cone free! I have so many cards they won't fit in my wallet. So I leave them at home, which means I have to get new ones whenever I walk into a shop.

Stores like giving out membership cards, because it encourages customer loyalty and makes shoppers feel like a privileged few getting a deal. "Congratulations. You are now a member of a Club anyone can join."

Cardholders like the idea because most of us could never get into a real club, and we're desperate to belong to anything.

The trend began with Club Price, where "members" could buy 100 bottles of shampoo for the price of 60 — as long as they have an airplane hangar to store them in. As Club Price's membership grew, everyone started offering cards.

Look in the phone book and you'll find hundreds of new clubs: Club Paper, Club Dry Cleaning, Club Carpet, Club Shoes, and Club Club. You can barely buy milk without joining the 2% Club.

Groucho Marx once said he wouldn't belong to any club that would have him as a member, but if he was around today, he wouldn't be able to go shopping.

The idea of discount "clubs" is new but the psychology has been around for a long time. My first "club" was a virtual secret society on the Main years ago, called Brown's department store. I went there at 18 with a friend and was about to pay the regular price for a pair of penny loafers when my friend whispered to the cashier: "Uhhh, Hotel Paris price, please."

The employee nodded meaningfully and deducted 25%. I never found out what the words meant, but I whispered them every time I shopped there for the next ten years. Hotel Paris was a secret password — the "Open Sesame" of shopping — and everyone who shopped at Brown's knew it, and felt very special.

Murray's Sports store downtown still runs the same way. I call it the "10% Club." To get the discount, you have to say: "*Pssst*. I get the special 10% discount." And everyone who shops at Murray's does.

Incredibly, many of the world's best-known hotel chains also work on this system. Walk into a big hotel and ask for a room and they'll charge you enough to buy it.

"A room with bath? Hmmm...well sir, That would be $1499 a night, plus tax and parking."

But tell the clerk you belong to an organization — any organization — and the price will fall immediately.

"You're a CAA member? That's 10% off, sir. Ohh, you're also a member of Windshield Wipers Anonymous — we'd be pleased to offer you another 15% off our regular price."

I usually request the "corporate rate," about 40% off, though I don't belong to a corporation. No matter. In fifteen years of travel and hundreds of hotels, no one has ever challenged me. It's like "Hotel Paris." Knowing the secret password is proof of club membership. Ask, and you get in, as long as you keep up with the latest code.

Several months ago, I was in Chicago and called hotels looking for a reasonable price. It was the weekend, and corporate rates were "not applicable." The prices were outrageous, so I called the Chicago tourist office for advice. The woman there practically burst out laughing when I told her what hotels were asking.

"They always pull that on first time vistors," she said."Just call the hotels back and say you want the "Weekend-with-the-Stars" special.

Most of them offer it."

"Great," I said."Who are the stars?"

"There aren't any," she said. "That's just the name they use for the special weekend price."

I called back the Best Western Hotel and seconds later the same clerk I had spoken to offered me a 50% discount. Every hotel I called reacted similarly. I knew the magic password — the "Hotel Paris" of Illinois — and Chicago was mine.

What worries me about this system is not what I know, but what I don't. What else works this way? Is there a secret password to buy half-price groceries at Loblaw's: "Open Sesame Crackers?"

Is there a Club Mercedes, offering half-price cars? A $3 Wine Club? A Club no GST? For all I know a whole class of people goes to $2 movies and eats $3 lobsters because they know the secret password.

I worry there are two classes of citizens — members and non-members — and I still don't have the right card.

JOSH.COM

❖

To CELEBRATE the new millennium, I've decided to reinvent myself. I'm tired of being plain old Josh Freed, columnist and journalist, and I'm ready to adapt to the times.

Welcome to Josh.com.

That little . at the end of my name may not seem like a big change to you, but it's the successful symbol of the 2000s, a million-dollar speck that's minimal but mighty. Putting a dot beside your name can increase your value a thousand times overnight.

Everywhere you turn people are making millions with a dot. Whether they're fresh out of college or just entering Pre-K. Such a high percentage of New Yorkers are dot-com millionaires that it must include some of the homeless.

Over 50% of North Americans say they know someone who has made a million dollars on a dot-com. That's why it's time you knew someone who became a millionaire too — and that person is me.

I want you to invest in me. I want my readers to become my backers, so I can go public and become a dot-com company too. With luck, we'll get me listed on the Toronto Stock Exchange and then on the NASDAQ — and pretty soon we'll all be rich.

What exactly will Josh.com do to make all this money? To be honest, I'm not sure yet. Right now, there's not a lot of need for a dot-com columnist, because most people still read newspapers. But the important thing is to get in first.

That way I will be way ahead of the pack whenever I figure out what it is I do — and the others will start emulating me.

Like all .com companies, the most important thing to do is create lots of buzz, but never actually make any money. That way the profits are all in the imagination of the investors, who buy the stock wildly, based on what it could become some day.

My model is amazon.com, the virtual bookstore whose president was recently named *Time*'s Man of the Year. Amazon doesn't actually own anything, or do anything but sell books on the internet, often at a higher price than you'd pay in a bookstore. It has lost half a billion dollars in five years, because most people still buy their books in a bookstore. But the company is worth a fortune because everyone's investing in it, dreaming of how many books it might sell some day.

In fact, the more money the company loses the more people buy stocks in it, thinking: "*Geez, if it's worth all that when it's losing money, imagine when it makes money! I better buy some stock before it's too late.*"

This is a ridiculous way to run a company. This is also the kind of company I want Josh.com to be, whatever it is it I eventually end up doing. For now, like all dot-coms I will have an exciting Web site filled with all my old columns, my new columns and even future column ideas to which you can contribute. If you like, you can even write my column.

I may also have a Josh.cam in my office where you can watch me scratch my head and pace for hours, as I write the column, then get desperate when the *Gazette* calls to ask me why it's late.

I will also have have ads on my site from relevant products such as smoked meat restaurants, hair growth clinics and of course, men's high fashion. All my services will be free, because that way I will draw more and more people to my website and increase my potential for the day I actually start doing something that could make money.

Don't worry. Like any smart.com I will do my best not to make a profit. Last Christmas, amazon.com made the terrible mistake of announcing their book sales had increased by 250% from the year before.

Soon after, their stock price plunged, as their shareholders stopped imagining fabulous future profits and started worrying about present ones. I guarantee this will not happen to me. If you invest in Josh.com, I foresee absolutely no profits in the coming years. Only ever-growing potential.

For those who worry about my age in an era of high school billionaires let me assure you that my senior vice president is a junior who is on the cutting edge of the ABC generation. My son Daniel, only four, already uses a computer and is learning to program the house VCR.

Better still, he cannot read so his mind is uncluttered by useless information. He is well on his way to becoming what is known as a "mouse potato." With his inexperience and my potential we are a succesful winning combination whose value can only go up. In fact if we are successful enough, we can raise Josh.com's value so high we do what every dot-com dreams up. We'll get bought out for a fortune by a huge dot-com column giant, like Dave Barry.

So get a piece of me now before you read in the *Wall Street Journal* about people who got rich on Josh. If Martha Stewart can do it so can I. Please help me use my potential. Send your cheque for Josh.com in today. At $3000 a share I am cheap and undervalued. I promise to spend the money as quickly as possible to make sure we're losing money and increasing my value.

Trust me. We're all going to be millionaires.

TWO

Just Joshing

TOMES YOU CAN TYPE ON

❖

I WAS WRITING on my laptop computer last week when I got a sudden pain in my lower back. I needed to raise my computer a few inches higher, so I reached for my usual all-purpose desk adjuster: Ariel and Will Durant's eleven-volume *The Story of Civilization*.

Volume 1, "Our Oriental Heritage," was 1,048 pages long and three inches thick — the perfect height to make my typing more comfortable.

These days, large offices spend a fortune on "ergonomic" chairs and desks that automatically adjust to precisely the right height, but I rely on the Durant system — a "handsomely-bound set" spanning 50,000 years and 10,000 pages. I also use the books as doorstops, paperweights and a stepladder for hard-to-reach lights and venetian blinds.

In theory, you can read the books, too, but I don't think many people do. Frankly, I think of them more as furniture than as literature. The Durant series is the kind of literature author Italo Calvino calls: The Books You've Been Planning to Read for Ages but Never Got Around To. He says you can usually find them on the same shelf as:

The Books You Read Decades Ago Which You Can't Remember Anything About, and the Books Everybody's Read so It's Almost as if You've Read Them Too.

Not to mention The Books You've Meant to Read For So Long You think You *HAVE* Read Them.

Almost everyone has this kind of dead lumber somewhere in their house. Other popular unfinished favorites include:

- The four-volume Selected Readings of Mao Tse-tung.
- The 1,000-page PBS companion volume to Vietnam.
- The Great Books of the World — a 60-volume history from Aristotle to Zoroaster, hyped for decades as filling an "ENTIRE FIVE-FOOT SHELF!"

I'm sure all of these are worthy and edifying books for those who have read them, but it's hard for most of us to find the time to read them.

Like millions of people, I bought the Durant set decades ago, as part of a "special introductory offer" from the Book-of-the-Month Club that advertised it as:

"The definitive history of the world!
"Normally $30,000 — now only $9.95!"

I was so excited I planned to read the entire series in a single 10,000-page sitting, but I never got past Page 118 of Volume 1, the start of the chapter on the Sumerians:

If we follow the Euphrates westward we shall find north and south of it the buried cities of ancient Sumeria: Eridu (now Abu Sharein), Ur (now Mukayyar), Uruk (Biblical Erech, now Warka), Larsa (Biblical Ellasar, now Senkereh), Lagash (now Shippurla).

I still plan to finish all eleven books someday, when I have a year's sabbatical, or join a monastery and take a lifetime vow of silence and reading.

Those of you who don't save Worthwhile Books probably save the TV equivalent: The Videos You Watched Part of Then Taped the Rest and Never Got Around to Finishing. Or The Videos You Thought You Taped That Ran Out of Tape Before You Finished Taping and Someday You'll Tape the Rest.

Some of you still have the entire NBA playoff series from Michael Jordan's last championship, except for the final quarter of the Last Game, or the 17-part environmental series on Protecting the Non-Furry Mammal.

The all-time unwatched classic of this kind is Ken Burns's series on the Civil War. Like half of North America you probably watched part of an episode, thought it was incredibly worthwhile to watch sometime, and taped the rest. Ever since, the entire 557-hour special has been sitting neatly on your shelf while you go out and rent the *Lion King* for the fifth time.

American video archivists estimate that Civil War tapes take up half the used videotape in North American homes, and some video environmentalists feel they should be seized by the government and erased in bulk. But like every information pack rat, you cling to your set. You know you should do something about it, but you can't erase the entire Civil War to record Wrestlemania, can you?

Well you're not alone. It's time you joined a growing support group: People Who Are Tired of Feeling Bad About the Shelves Full of Worthwhile Stuff They Mean to Watch or Read Anonymous.

I joined the group a few years ago when I was recovering from my own experience with scientist Stephen W. Hawking's book, *A Brief History of Time*. Like millions of people, I'd bought the book thinking it could explain the origins of the universe to a scientific dimwit like me. But halfway through it, the universe seemed far more complicated than ever, because of paragraphs like this:

> In addition to the photon there were 3 other spin-1 particles known collectively as massive vector bosons . . . called W + W- and Z naught and each had a mass of about 100 GeV (giga-electron-volts).

The book sat on my shelf for two years making me feel stupider and guiltier every time I picked it up, and then quickly put it down. Then, one day, I found out that publishers refer to Hawking's book as a UBS, an Unexplained Best-Seller.

Apparently, the book's own distributors were so curious about its popularity they put $5 coupons near the end of one thousand copies. None of the coupons were ever redeemed, which means there were millions of people just like me.

For all I know there's a $5 coupon somewhere in my 11-volume Durant series, too, and a 5-yuan note in my Mao Tse-Tung collection. I'll probably never get far enough to find out but at least I don't feel bad about it anymore.

Occasionally, I think I should cart my Durants, the Hawking and my other Worthwhile Books off to a library, only I suspect they'd get even less use there. Not only would they sit unread on the shelves, but no one would use them to adjust the height of their desk.

KNOT ME

❖

IF YOU RUN INTO ME at a black-tie affair, I'm easy to spot: just look for the guy with the naked neck. I know the tie is part of the standard male uniform, a useful costume for sneaking into clubs or weddings where you haven't been invited. But any place that would accept me in a tie isn't a place I care to be invited.

I know many men wear ties because they like to, or because they have to, but most wear them because everyone else does. Women generally wear clothing to be noticed, but guys wear things so we won't be noticed, and a tie is a good way of joining the army of the invisible.

It's not my way. For me the necktie is the *chador* of male fashion, the Japanese foot-binding of men's clothes, the gallows of the sartorial world. And I speak from long experience.

My resentment goes back to childhood when the tie was a mandatory school uniform that never seemed to suit my style. I wore one every day of my high-school life and felt like a prisoner in ill-fitting clothing. In class photos I usually look like I've just been lynched. There's a bluish tint to my face and I seem to be struggling for air, only natural when you look at the noose around my neck.

The ties in these photos never look quite right: they hang slightly off centre, or over my shoulder, or outside my collar, or someplace else they don't belong. Usually they are stained by ink, grape juice, or whatever else was in my lunchbox that day. They are crowned by an aptly named "knot" — a twisted, frayed thing that looks like it's been used to secure a sailboat. In fact, because of the tie, I have few childhood shots where I don't look ridiculous.

My dad tried vainly to improve my tie-tying technique. I recall him standing patiently with me by the mirror, teaching me the subtle difference between the Windsor knot and the straight one. But somehow, mine always looked like a reef knot.

It was the mirror that partly thwarted my efforts, since I am directionally-challenged. My hand went one way in the mirror and my tie went the other in reality, and the next thing I knew it was hanging down forlornly in another knot that took ten minutes to undo. I spent so much time trying to get the damn thing off they should have called it an "untie."

I arrived at university in the 1960s just as the dress code was disappearing, and suddenly I was liberated. My woman friends were ready to burn their bras, but I was an arsonist with a different dream. Ahhh! those heady years of university; the wind against my neck, the freedom of the open collar. Josh Unbound!

In school the tie was a symbol of the establishment, and we tore them off like chains. But once we had graduated and needed jobs, they became golden chains that were hard to resist. In the 1970s I went to work at a newspaper, where ties were again the team uniform. Later, when I went to work on TV, my CBC television bosses explained that "everyone on TV wears ties — and so will you."

I tried to argue but the rule was so unshakable you'd have thought televisions didn't work without ties, that they were part of the antenna. I bought two pathetic striped ties and put them on whenever I did a "stand-up," but I looked as uncomfortable as in my Grade Three photo.

My employers wanted me to look like all the other reporters, but instead I looked like I was impersonating a reporter. And even my bosses knew it. I still remember a senior Toronto producer calling me into his office one day to watch a video of my latest story. Part way through the tape he froze the frame and stabbed a finger at the screen "Isn't that your tie?" he said, pointing at my neck.

"Yes," I said defiantly. "So?"

"So, it's OUTSIDE your collar!"

He stabbed the screen again. "And what's that?" he demanded, pointing at a blotchy looking spot on my collar. "I could swear it's a mustard stain!"

From then on, they assigned a fastidious producer to examine me before every stand-up, like my mother did when I was ten. He made sure my tie was always tied correctly, as tightly as a noose. I began to think that men died younger than women because they'd been slowly strangled to death; that science would someday discover that ties cut off oxygen to the brain and slowly executed you; that neckties would be remembered in the history books as "a primitive custom of the masochistic second millennium."

So why *do* men wear them?

Not surprisingly, the tie is of military origin. It dates back to the 1600s, when Croatian mercenaries showed up in France wearing linen scarves round their necks. Fashion-conscious Parisians liked the idea and began to wear similar neckwear, knotted in the centre with flowing ends.

The French called the thing a *cravate* — their name for the Croats who inspired it. The fad spread to England, where fashion-conscious King Charles II liked it so much he made the tie mandatory in court, and I guess it's been mandatory ever since — a functionless, un-comfortable piece of attire that's made many a man miserable.

I made my stand against it in the early 1980s. One day I just stopped wearing a tie on TV and waited to fight it out with my producers, but none of them ever told me to put it back on. I guess they finally realized that I looked far more normal without a tie than I did with one.

I haven't worn a tie since — like a man who has escaped prison and never wants to go back. Today, my trademark is my bare neck, and times are catching up with me. Casual Fridays are increasingly common at work, and they're spreading to become casual Monday-through-Fridays.

Even TV news has loosened the rules. Today you see many reporters exposing their necks on the small screen, without disrupting transmission. In fact, reporters routinely appear in sweaters and even T-shirts, as do rock stars and Wall Street attorneys. Stephen Spielberg wears plaid work shirts to his movie openings and President Bill Clinton wears jogging shorts and a baseball cap.

I am on the cusp of fashion.

The tie as mandatory uniform may finally be dying and if it does I'd like to think it was partly because of me; that I was one of those who sparked the revolution and helped cut the ties that bind us.

IF THE SUIT DOESN'T FIT

❖

WHEN I'M TRAVELING, I like to bring home something unusual to help me recall my trip: a scroll, carving or other memento that inevitably winds up in a box in my shed. So when I was in Hong Kong recently toward the end of a long trip, I looked around for a souvenir that would last.

Hong Kong is the clothing capital of Asia where every back alley is filled with cheap knockoffs of name-brand clothing, from $10 Polo shirts to $20 Nikes. It's a city of tailors, and many seemed to be short of work; they stood in front of small shops on every second street corner, hawking tailored suits and jackets like vendors selling pretzels in New York.

"Sir, perhaps you would like to buy a suit that's made-to-measure?" said one typical gentleman, dressed in elegant pinstripes. "It will fit you as well as the suit you wore the day you were born."

I don't have much need for suits or even jackets, and when I do, I buy them off the rack at The Bay, because a size 42 jacket fits me perfectly. But standing amidst the bustle of Hong Kong, I found myself wondering what it would be like to have a suit made just for me.

For years I'd read about made-to-measure suits in Graham Greene and John Le Carré novels, so the prospect of owning one seemed almost romantic. After a short search, I chose a tailor shop near my hotel: a tiny place about five feet deep, called Royal Canny Tailor Men's Suitings, and Mr. Liu was the canny fellow who ran it.

He was a roundish gentleman whose father had once owned an elegant shop in the heart of downtown, until Hong Kong's real-estate boom forced the family to relocate to more modest quarters.

"Our new shop is very small," said Mr.Liu, "but our talent is still very big."

Buying a jacket off the rack in a Canadian store is simple enough. You wander around looking at jackets until you see something you like, then you hope they have your size. But getting a made-to-measure suit is more demanding. First, Mr. Liu and his aging tailor took my measurements with a yellowed tape, then they pulled out an immense pile of fabrics.

"Which ones do you like?" asked Mr. Liu, thumbing through them rapidly, like a cashier counting currency. "We have wool, synthetic wool, polywool, polyester, suede, piqué, cashmere, crepe, mohair, and micro-fibre."

He riffled through another pile of swatches, baffling me further with a huge choice of colours, shades and patterns that came in tweeds, twills, checks, and stripes. Who knew what I wanted? The swatches were so small it was hard to imagine them in a jacket so big.

After a half-hour of deliberation, I picked what Mr. Liu called an "Italian charcoal check polywool gabardine," and breathed a sigh of relief. Yet it was just the start of my task.

Did I want a jacket with two, three or four buttons? Half-lining or full lining? Padded shoulders or dropped? Would it be single or double-breasted? With vents or without? And what kind of pockets did I want: flap, flapless or the new "jet pockets" that Mr. Liu assured me were "very fashionable with Hong Kong gentlemen these days."

"Just regular pockets, please," I said in a rare burst of decisiveness. "You know, the kind that hold pens."

Making my own jacket seemed as complicated as building my own house. The male suit may look like a dull, standard uniform, but to make it dull is one of the most elaborate tasks on the planet. A woman's suit often has only ten or fifteen parts to stitch together, but a man's jacket can contain up to eighty pieces, and I seemed to be choosing them all. Not to mention the pants, which involved choices about cuffs, pleats, inseams and more.

By the time I left the shop that morning I was worn out, though Mr. Liu assured me the hardest part was over. All that remained was "the final fitting" that night.

At ten p.m. I was back in his shop, the emerging jacket draped over me like a shroud. It looked like a cross between a scarf and a potato sack, but Mr. Liu assured me it was just the clay from which art would emerge. Meanwhile, his tailor drew chalk marks all over the "jacket," as he tugged at my sleeves, tightened threads and stuck needles in me as if I were a mannequin.

"You come back tomorrow night at seven p.m.," said Mr. Liu at last, after fifteen minutes of modeling. "Your suit will be ready."

When I arrived next evening, my jacket and pants were, indeed, ready. I tried them on and looked in the mirror, where the suit looked pretty good until I turned around and looked at the back. The whole jacket was crinkled, and a thick lump of material was bunched up from the back of my neck to the bottom of my shoulderblades. I looked like the hunchback of Hong Kong.

Mr. Liu dismissed the problem as a small "wrinkle" and had his tailor iron the jacket for a good ten minutes. Nothing changed. My plane was leaving Hong Kong at five a.m. and the only way I could wear the jacket was if I kept my back to the wall.

"OK, OK, no problem," said Mr. Liu. "You come back at midnight tonight, and I open shop special for you. Everything be fine, you'll see."

12:15 a.m. Five hours before my flight, I paced to and fro on a dark, lonely street outside the Royal Canny Tailor shop. I'd been there ten minutes but it was still locked up tight, causing me many doubts. Had Mr. Liu forgotten our rendezvous? Or had he simply given up and gone to sleep, choosing to keep my half-price deposit and forget the suit? Had I been taken to the tailor's?

Then, in the darkness, I saw Mr. Liu and his old tailor trudging toward me, clutching the now-familiar garment. They let me into the shop and silently slipped on the jacket. The crinkles were gone, the hump had vanished; only the collar was still lumpy. The tailor spent several more minutes diligently pressing it and the lump got slightly smaller. Mr. Liu sighed and gamely offered to send the tailor back for a final effort. I could pick up the jacket at three a.m. on my way to the airport.

I looked at the bags under Mr. Liu's eyes and the bigger ones under the old tailor's.

"It's fine" I said, adding to myself: "If the suit doesn't fit, wear it anyways." And five hours later, I was on a flight home, the suit tucked into my luggage.

Next day I unwrapped my purchase eagerly and tried it on with fresh eyes, and to be fair, it's not bad-looking. But I've come to the conclusion that made-to-measure suits are made for another era, when people had the time, care and money to make them just right—and I don't. I'm sure that with a few more visits, fittings and adjustments, Mr. Liu's jacket would have fit me perfectly, maybe even as well as a size 42 from The Bay.

MANLY ME

❖

LIKE ALL DISASTERS it started innocently, as I backed into a parking spot and felt my car hit the curb. When I got out, my front tire was already flat. It was Sunday night at 11:15 p.m., and no tow trucks would be on the road, but I took the situation like a man.

In my twenties I had a series of jalopies which I sometimes fixed, because repairing them at a garage would have cost more than the cars. Besides, tinkering with cars boosted my male pride, even though I wasn't very adept. Once, I spent a few days ripping apart my engine and then reassembling it, only to find there was a big piece leftover on the ground: a cylinder ring that belonged inside.

In recent years I haven't done car repairs because I have a newer model that rarely has problems. But like many men, I take pride in the fact that I could fix something if I had to. So as I watched the air escaping my tire, I saw a challenge — it had been years since I'd changed a tire, but I could do it in the dark. In fact, I'd have to, because it *was* dark.

I opened the trunk to get out the jack and suddenly remembered that spare tires aren't really tires anymore, just those silly mini-tires meant to get you to a garage mechanic. The jack was a tiny, designer contraption bolted aesthetically into the bottom of my trunk. It obviously popped out of the trunk somehow, but how? I pulled on the jack. I yanked it. I smashed it with a hammer. It didn't budge. There were tiny instructions on the side of the jack but my eyesight isn't what it was and I didn't have my reading glasses. Still, I knew I could do this; I NEEDED to do this for my male ego which was deflating faster than my tire.

I opened the glove compartment and pulled out the 300-page car manual to see if it had a "Dummy's Guide to Taking the Jack Out of the Car, Stupid." But unfortunately, since I live in Quebec, the manual was in French only — and I had no clue how to say "jack" in French. I tried "Jacques," with no luck. Then I held the manual up to the dim car dome light and worked my way through 150 pages of text before stumbling on the right section.

As I'm sure you know, the French word for jack is *cric*, which is what

I had in my neck from trying to read the manual by roof light.

Ten minutes later, carefully following the French instructions, I managed to pry *le cric* from *le trunk* and was ready to go to work on *le pneu*. It was 12:05 a.m and cold as I kneeled in the snow, and peered into the darkness under my car.

Today's cars don't have bumpers you can just jack up. You have to fit the tiny special jack into a tiny special slot under the car, which I couldn't see in the dark. I crawled under the car in the sopping wet snow and peered about with my flashlight, until my hat fell off into a puddle, and sank. But at last I saw the slot. As I slithered out from under the car on my back, I felt triumphant, until I heard a snarl and felt two paws stab my chest hard. A furry face lunged at my throat, and I froze in terror.

Then, I heard a shrill voice: "Freddy, No! Bad dog. Bad. Bad!"

A young woman emerged from the darkness and the creature backed off. It was a German Shepherd, which suddenly looked contrite. I looked in shock at the woman, expecting an apology, but all she said was, "I think you startled him." Then she and her hound disappeared into the night.

It took a minute for my heart to stop pounding in my chest, then I went to work unscrewing the tire bolts. To protect myself from the wet snow, I unfastened my son's tiny child seat and lay it over the curbside. I sat in it like an oversized five-year old, as passersby giggled.

Changing a tire is a lot more complex than when I owned a $200 junkheap. Nowadays, tires have fancy hubcaps that don't come off *until* the bolts are out. But you can't get at the bolts because the hub cap is in the way. It took ten minutes to unscrew one tire bolt, bending my hub cap like a sardine can. Ten minutes later, I had the second bolt out and was proudly working on a third when I noticed something bizarre. My flat tire was as hard as a rock again. It was a miracle! — my tire had magically refilled with air! I paused to think through the puzzle and came to a horribly embarrassing realization that I'd never tell anyone but you.

In my post-*cric*, post-dog-attack confusion, I had made a small mistake: I was removing the wrong tire. A wave of humiliation rushed over me, shredding what little remained of my male pride. I cursed myself and punched the snow. It was 12:35 a.m. and a bitter wind swept across my exposed head.

My hair was wet, my ears frozen and my ego shrivelled, but I was too far in to quit now. Besides, what else could possibly go wrong — aside from the car falling and crushing me after I'd jacked it up?

In despair, I began screwing the bolts back into the good tire. I got one bolt in and was starting on the second when it slipped from my frozen fingers and fell on the ground between my knees. I peered down but couldn't see it. It had obviously rolled against the curb, but when I looked there with my flashlight, there was no bolt. In fact, there was no curb, only a gaping hole in the curb.

That's when I made my final embarrassing discovery. Throughout the "repairs," I had unknowingly been sitting atop a sewer — and had dropped the tire bolt directly into it. I sat there in silence for a longer time than I remember. I thought about how foolish I felt and about my lost pride. I thought about my fancy hubcaps, my primitive skills and my Utter Failure to be A Man. Then I realized there was one tool I was actually very adept with—the phone. At one a.m. I trudged into the house, dialed a garage and quickly arranged to have my car towed in next morning, while I was at work. It was a far easier and more natural task for me than changing a tire, except for one difficult moment.

"So which tire needs repair?" asked the mechanic.

"Uh, well," I mumbled. "There are actually two tires with a problem. One has a flat and the other is missing...a bolt."

"A bolt!?" said the surprised mechanic. "How the heck did you lose that?"

"Someone stole it," I said curtly and hung up before he asked more questions. After all, a guy's got to do something to preserve his pride in being a man.

JEWISH SANTA

❖

I WAS WANDERING down St. Laurent Boulevard singing aloud, when I suddenly realized with embarrassment what tune I was belting out:

You'd better not shout, you'd better not frown,
Santa Claus is coming to to-o-o-wn!

This may seem like an odd tune for a nice Jewish boy to be singing, but I've had a love-hate relationship with Christmas for decades. Like most Jewish kids in Montreal, I attended Protestant-run schools and got indoctrinated into Christmas at a tender age.

By seven, I was playing a shepherd in the school Christmas play, and by ten I'd learned all the words to the Christmas carol classics: "Silent Night," "Deck the Halls with Boughs of Holly," and my favorite tune, "O Come All Ye Faithful," which I crooned at the breakfast table throughout Christmas, stunning my mother when I came to the finale:

O Come let us ado-ore hi-i-im
Chri-i-ist the lord!

My parents did their best to keep up my Christmas cheer, despite the obvious absence of Christ in our home. We didn't celebrate the holiday, but we went to an annual Christmas/Hanukkah party at some Protestant friends, where we ate turkey and Yorkshire pudding accompanied by bagels and potato knishes.

Who knew I was living in a dream?

When I left high school, I suddenly found I had left Christmas too. At university, no one sang Christmas carols in class, and I didn't get much chance to sing them anywhere else. There were no Christmas/Hanukkah parties anymore either and Christmas suddenly became a lonely time for those who didn't celebrate.

To make things worse, Quebec law seemed to punish you if you didn't have a party to go to. Bars and most restaurants were forced to close at midnight December 24 and couldn't re-open for two days. While most families celebrated, I walked the city's deserted streets a homeless Christmas person in search of some good cheer. I felt like the X in Xmas, and I didn't like it.

In my youth I'd been imbued with the corny Christmas magic and I still cried every time I watched *Miracle on 34th Street*. I had a romantic conception of Christmas, but where could I find it again?

When I became a journalist I went on a relentless quest for Christmas. While other reporters were home eating their Christmas turkey, I prowled the streets interviewing the homeless or hanging around the Old Brewery Mission. One year, I convinced Eaton's to let me replace their store Santa for a day. I dressed up in a red suit and eighteen pounds of padding and spent the day as Eaton's first Jewish Santa.

Hundreds of kids sat on my lap eyeing me like an imposter, but I wasn't worried. Eaton's real Santa had taught me his No. 1 rule: "Always hold their hands affectionately as soon as they sit down. That way they can't pull off your beard.'"

Most of the kids wanted TVs, stereos, flying carpets, or popular brand names like "Evel Knievel's Motorcycle." However, I didn't promise them anything because their parents always whispered their orders in my ear.

"Tell her she's getting a Barbie doll. Don't promise anything we can't afford!" said one father. "Last year you promised our son a Fleetwood Cadillac — and we fought all Christmas morning. You do that again and I'll have you fired."

It was a demoralizing experience, but I didn't give up my Christmas addiction easily. Later, as a TV reporter for CBC in the 1980s, I went on a nationwide quest for Christmas, visiting a different Christmas event in every province over the twelve days of Christmas.

I danced till dawn with masqueraded mummers in Newfoundland. I joined a gospel choir at a Halifax prison. I flew to remote settlements on the West Coast in a helicopter with "The Flying Santa" of the Coast Guard, and I joined Vancouver's Christmas-light boat flotilla as it toured the harbor. I ended up on a yacht with several drunken millionaires guzzling champagne and eggnog and crooning "Jingle Bell Rock."

My cross-country Christmas journey left me disappointed, too, until I dropped in on an orphanage in St. John's, Newfoundland, where I finally felt I had found the spirit of Kris Kringle. The orphanage was holding its annual Christmas draw and poor young orphans right out of a Hollywood movie were winning prizes and thanking the priests who cared for them with wide-eyed appreciation. On CBC national TV I interviewed several of the youngsters and announced I had finally found Christmas in this "touching" human event.

It was touching in more ways than I knew. Shortly after my report, news broke that the Mount Cashel orphanage was a haven for priests who abused children. I felt like a Christmas turkey for seeing what I wanted to at that institution instead of what I should have — and it finally put an end to my romantic quest for Christmas.

Today, I accept Christmas for what it is: a sometimes happy, often annoying and frequently lonely event for those who don't participate. Gradually, I've learned a few non-Christian tricks for coping with the season. On Christmas Eve I go to first-run movies because they're always empty. On Christmas Day, I go skiing because nobody is on the hills except a few other people with no place to go.

I watch some Christmas specials on TV, hum some carols and try to see the windowful of mechanical toys at Ogilvy's at least once. Strangely, now that I expect less of Christmas, I probably enjoy it more than most people. I avoid the expectations and disappointments that seem to afflict so many of my Christian friends during this season. I have no obligations.

Sometimes when I'm downtown, I feel a touch of envy for the crowds of Christmas shoppers passing by, buying gifts for their loved ones. But I know I'll have my own buying spree later. That's why Boxing Day and post-Christmas sales were invented, so us non-Christians can go shopping when everyone else is broke.

MR. DON'T-FIX-IT

❖

THE LOCK ON MY FRONT DOOR had gotten so rusty I needed vise grips to turn the key. The cheapest locksmith I could find wanted $40 for a house call, and it seemed like a waste of money. The lock was just a cheap deadbolt, attached to the door by a few screws. It looked easy to remove and take over to the locksmith — but for me it was as intimidating as brain surgery.

Guys are supposed to be handymen who know nuts from bolts and other things, but I've never had mechanical genes. My hands have the fine-motor ability of a penguin's flippers. My brain has the natural mechanical instinct of a bear handed a fishing rod. My friends call me "Mr. Don't-Fix-It," because anytime I do fix something, it ends up more broken.

I've always resented those Mr. Fix-It types who can repair anything the moment it breaks. Your beach chair snaps at the ocean, and they pull a Swiss army knife out of their bathing trunks and snap it back together with their portable riveter.

Not that I wouldn't like to be like them. At various times in my life I've tried to get in touch with my "Inner Handyman." I took an auto-mechanics course in college and learned the names of all the things I couldn't fix. So now at least I can talk like a regular guy: "Yup, looks like the starter solenoid shorting out the grommet rod sump-pump and the gasket seal driveshaft nimrod torque ring."

I once volunteered to help some friends who were renovating their house, figuring I'd learn some handy skills. But after a few hours of work, they politely suggested the best way I could help was to leave. Even my mother has stopped asking for my help. One evening I carefully hung up a big Inuit painting she'd received as a gift. The next evening it crashed to the ground, shattering the glass into a thousand pieces, along with a lovely clay pot from India.

So over the years I've gradually stopped repairing anything, which seems to suit everyone. My spouse won't even tell me where the tool chest is. She wields the hammer in our household, though sometimes she lets me hold the nails.

All this is not without some guilt. Deep inside, my Inner Handyman hisses his contempt, taunting me for my inadequacy. "Why can't you be a real man? Why can't you change a sparkplug, washer, or lightbulb?

"What are you, a man or a klutz?"

And so the broken door lock beckoned like a chance at redemption, after a lifetime of humiliation. It was 1 p.m. and I had a long day of writing ahead of me, but it would take less than a half-hour to get the job done. I found a screwdriver, undid four screws, and seconds later the lock fell right into my hand.

Pleased with myself, I headed off to the locksmith where the man behind the counter said my lock was in good working order; all it needed was a new "cylinder barrel." He slipped one in, charged me $19 and handed me back the lock.

"Just pop her back in the same way she came out and it should last you for years," he said.

More confident by the moment, I went home and screwed the lock back into the door. To be certain that there were no problems, I tested it a few times with the door open, and it worked perfectly. I felt a flush of pride — I had actually *fixed* something and I'd saved $37, too! Maybe an old dog could learn new tricks.

I began to think of other things that needed repairing around the house. Our coffeemaker hadn't worked for weeks. My computer printer had been on the fritz for months. The CD player had broken three years ago. Maybe I could even build a deck, like other guys did, and wear one of those belts around my hips with tape measures and drills hanging off it. Josh the Renovater. Reno-Josh.

Dreaming of my future deck, I closed the front door and locked it. Then I turned the key to re-enter the house, but for some reason, it didn't work this time. It just spun round and round in the cylinder. I fiddled with it, then gently jiggled it, because I didn't know what else to do. I couldn't take the lock apart again unless I got back into the house.

I tried to remain calm and rational — then I went into a fury. I rammed my shoulder against the door and kicked it with all my might, but it was as solid as a bank vault.

For the next ninety minutes, I tried to break into my house. I went around back and clambered up the fire escape, then leapt onto the balcony. But all the windows were locked. My house was as secure as Fort Knox, which was reassuring if I could ever get inside.

At 4:30 p.m., four hours after I'd started fixing the door, I arrived back at the lock shop and explained my situation. The staff tried to look sympathetic and contain their smirks. They said I'd need a locksmith to pick the lock, but there wasn't one available until night. He cost $62 an hour.

What could I do? I went home and prowled around, waiting for him, trying to look like I was in charge, instead of what I felt like. Stupid. At seven p.m., the locksmith arrived, a solid guy in his forties who looked like one of those Mr. Fix-It types. He worked at the lock a while but couldn't pick it, so he had to break in.

He ripped out the new cylinder barrel with big pliers and replaced it ($35). He smashed out the old lock with a hammer and screwdriver and put in a new one ($55). He drilled a huge new hole in my door and repaired the holes he had smashed ($45). The total bill came to $155, not to mention five hours lost from my work day and a year lost from my life in aggravation.

Still, I'm trying to look on the bright side. Watching him work, I learned something important about repairing door locks: a locksmith does it better than me. Just as other specialists do other things better.

I'm going back to being Mr. Don't-Fix-it. Next time I have to change a lightbulb, I'm calling an electrician.

THE NAMING GAME

❖

I RECENTLY READ that France's government had barred a baby girl from having the name Fleur de Marie because it wasn't on the country's "official" list of Roman Catholic saint names.

This isn't the first time the French have made news by vetoing a child's name. In the past, they've nixed the names Manhattan, Cherry and Prune, not to mention Klafouti, a name inspired by the father's favorite baked fruit dish.

Like Quebec, France doesn't allow you to give a child a ridiculous name, but the French seem to take the law to ridiculous lengths. Then again, they're practically easygoing compared with the Germans. The clerks who register names in Germany will refuse any name that confuses the sexes (like Leslie), or sounds strange in another country (like Goofy), or just sounds strange to them (like Josh, if you live in Germany).

Among the many names German clerks have rejected are Woodstock, Pushkin, Martinlutherking and Moewe, the German word for seagull. Meanwhile, the German parliament includes members with popular names like Herta Daeubler-Gmelin and Heidimaarie Wieczorek-Zeul.

Not that I have particularly daring taste when it comes to names. Over the decades, I've argued with friends who wanted to name their kids Stardust, Breeze and Fidel and I'd oppose anyone who tried to name their kid something equally hip today, like Big Mac, or Stair-Master, or Yo (though YoYo is fine with me).

In the end, I believe the name is a parent's decision. The government won't change their kids' diapers, so why should it change their names? Besides, a strange name isn't really likely to ruin your life. I've met kids named Africa, Sunshine, Moonbeam and Toke and they didn't seem unhappy to me. And I've known kids with perfectly dull names who suddenly got stuck with school nicknames like Iggy, Bugsy and Fish.

In the sixties, many people of my generation got tired of the usual names like John and Mary and changed them to cooler ones like Sky and Earth. So if kids don't like their names today, they can always change them to something they think is cooler—like Butthead, or John, or Mary.

I suspect that names are usually more traumatic for parents than they are for kids. My son turned one year old yesterday and I'm only starting to get over the nightmare of naming him.

When he was born we called him The Kid for a long time, because we couldn't agree on a name. My wife wanted to call him Justin, I preferred Louie. Her second choices were Jonah and Nicholas, mine were Mickey and Jake. I liked Gus and Hank; she wanted Richard and Julius. We both liked Woody, but no one else did.

"You can't call a child Woody!" people screamed. "Kids will tease him for being a woodpecker."

Everyone seemed to have an opinion. In one of my columns, I'd mentioned The Kid, and soon I was getting angry letters demanding I give him a "real" name—from readers who'd probably be more comfortable with French or German rules.

Meanwhile, the government deadline for choosing a name was approaching. Quebec is looser than France about what you call your kid, as long you call him something. If a child doesn't have a name after 30 days, they fine you $50 and they can even decide to pick a name for you. What would that turn out to be here in Quebec in the late nineties?

Lucien?

As the deadline approached, we scoured books of popular names. I even combed the Bible from Adam to Zacharias, but the good names seemed to be overused, and the rest sounded old-fashioned. Would you name your kid Lemuel? Or Esau? Or Ezekiel?

I also checked a book of people with real, but remarkable names. My favorites included Iona Victory Bond, Justin Time, John Senior Junior, Ura Hogg (and his wife Ima), and Warren Peace.

Eventually a gang of friends came over to help us out of the dilemma and they suggested dozens of different names. "I've got it!" screamed one. "How about ... Oscar?"

"Ugh!" said another. "That was the name of my uncle, the bigamist ... but how about Felix?"

"Felix?" said another. "That's the name of my cat."

It left my wife and me more confused.

Finally, a month was up since our son had been born. At four p.m. on a Friday afternoon, with a few minutes to go to the deadline, I rushed into a government office and told the clerk our last-minute choice.

Daniel Harry — D.H. for short.

"Daniel" wasn't either of our first picks but it had squeaked into both our Top 10 lists. It was also bilingual, it even worked in Spanish, and it sure beat Lucien. Harry was my dad's name.

However, for me, the confusion still wasn't over. As the months went by, I couldn't get used to calling The Kid by name. He seemed too immature for such an adult name, too Louie-ish to be a Daniel. I kept trying out other names, hoping to find a nickname that would stick. Some days I called him Dimitri, or Luigi, or Igor. Other times it was Woody or D.H.

However, in recent months, I'm finally coming round to liking his name, so I guess he's growing into it. Or more likely I am. On his birthday, we sang "Happy Birthday Daniel," and he looked pretty happy, but frankly, he looks happy when you call him just about anything, as long as you're offering food.

I figure he can always decide how he feels about being a Daniel when he's older. If he doesn't like it, he can change it to something he prefers, like Klafouti. Or The Kid.

HOUSEWARMING FROM HELL

❖

IT's STRANGELY THRILLING to watch a fire, especially when it's happening at your own house. I discovered this last week during an unexpected real-life thriller I think of as "Backdraft on Esplanade Ave."

We'd arrived home from hospital three days earlier with "The Kid," our still nameless baby son, but we hadn't expected his greeting to be quite so warm. It started just after breakfast last Wednesday as I was reading the morning papers. I heard a siren, then saw a firetruck pull up outside our flat.

Hmmm, what's up?, I wondered, poking my head out the window. Was there a fire someplace in the area? Seconds later, my heart stopped — the fire was next door. Smoke was pouring out the third-floor flat beside our kitchen and flames were coming our way across the common roof. Smoke was streaming out our back shed, so we did what came naturally — and panicked.

My wife frantically bundled up The Kid, while I rushed out onto the balcony and pulled boxes of old paper out of the shed before they ignited. I'd barely finished when someone appeared at our door: a yellow-outfitted fireman with a terse message: "We have to evacuate you in a few minutes. Gather what you think is important while there's still time."

They say that at moments like this, you discover what you value most in life, so I guess I value only one thing — paper. I have an awesome thirty-year collection of paper scraps: a vast storeroom collection of newspaper articles, scrapbooks, screenplays, letters, 1979 receipts, 1972 tax files, 1966 postcards and other even more precious material.

There is my master list of favorite cheap Montreal restaurants, culled over three decades; my high school report cards and compositions; my first, and last, poem; not to mention a thousand birthday cards, phone numbers, bus transfers and other memorabilia it would take me years to sift through and file.

This wasn't the time. I flung pile after pile of paper into giant boxes, like someone shovelling coal into a train engine, and quickly filled seven cartons. Meanwhile, my wife grabbed what mattered most to her: two photo albums and one child.

Most of our possessions didn't matter to either of us:VCRs, toasters, TVs, and sofas seemed meaningless.We had insurance and our furniture wasn't worth anything anyway. I opened a closet, looked at my clothing and closed it.Why rescue one sweater, or pair of socks?

With the help of our next-door neighbor Gerry, we carried The Kid and the boxes outside.The last I saw of my house, four firemen were rushing into our bedroom with axes. Fifteen minutes later the house beside ours was in flames. 100 firemen swarmed over our roof with ladders and hoses, trying to stop the blaze from spreading.

I watched with a large crowd as huge clouds of smoke billowed over my building and obscured our house from view. It looked like the living room was ablaze and I thought of more things I should have taken: the paintings, wood carvings and other knick-knacks I'd gathered on trips around the world, including a collection of one-dollar wooden elephants gathered on five continents. I would miss them when we moved into a new elephant-free house.

Suddenly the smoke lifted and my spirits lifted, as I saw teams of firemen still on my roof, spraying everything in sight. My priorities had changed fast: an hour earlier, the sight of firemen on my roof was terri-fying; now it was a relief. It meant I still had a roof for them to stand on!

I spent most of the day watching the fire from a red mobile bus shelter the City makes available to fire victims. My neighbors and I sat in it, drinking coffee and filling out fire reports.Volunteers from a local youth agency offered us a free hotel and food voucher. Reporters buzzed about with cameras asking "How do you feel?"— but few of us felt like talking.

A neighbor whose home had been destroyed sat alone in a corner of the bus and sobbed quietly. But soon the fire was under control and by evening it was out. The building beside ours was in ruins but ours was still standing, only how much damage would we find when we returned?

We'd reserved a hotel room for the night but waited around to see our flat. At eight p.m., the fire marshal gave me the green light, along with a wink of his eye.

"I think you'll be surprised," he said.

The shed and part of our back balcony was gone, while the back yard was a mess of burnt timber. Our roof was leaking in several places, half the bedroom wall was down and smoke was everywhere, but frankly, our home had never looked as good. Sure, there was a big hole in the bedroom ceiling where we could see the roof — but why not look at the bright side? We'd been thinking of getting a skylight anyway.

I felt an enormous mix of feelings: fatigue, gratitude to the City of Montreal firemen, relief that The Kid had lived through the most exciting day he was likely to have for years — and slept through all of it. He could always catch up on the day later in life. He'd been filmed by a CBC camera crew as we rushed him down the front stairs in his small basket. Four days old and he'd made the evening news.

Now that's what I call a housewarming.

GRAVE TROUBLE

❖

IT'S NOT EVERY VACATION that I get involved with grave robbers, so let me tell you about my recent mid-east travels and The Tale of the Stolen Syrian Statue.

We'd come to Syria out of curiousity and found it to be a sort of Disneyland-for-dictators, still ruled by President Hafez Assad. The country was completely cut off from the western world: there were no Mcdonald's, Pizza Huts or other brand name stores you see almost everywhere on the globe nowadays. The only pervasive brand was President Assad, whose portrait hung over every falafel stand, carpet shop, bus stop, building and bridge. Yet the country's outlaw status had advantages for visitors like us.

Syria's 6,000 years of history provide some of the world's most spectacular ruins and you don't have to share them with busloads of tourists. We'd spent a week in Damascus and now we'd hired a burly driver named Omar to take us into the countryside to two of Syria's most famous ruins.

The first was Afamia, where Omar dropped us in the middle of nowhere at a breathtaking two-mile row of Roman arches. He said he'd meet us at the other end of the colonnade in two hours time, and soon we were wandering alone through a 20-foot high row of ancient stone columns. The place had a haunting stillness, that was suddenly broken by a loud voice: "Hey mister! You want to buy antiques. I find in tomb yesterday."

Behind some pillars a man in an Arab headscarf was holding up several dusty coins that bore faded Roman faces. Then again, maybe they were fakes he had made at home that morning — who knew? Two men on an old motorscooter pulled out from behind another pillar bearing bigger treasure: two sculpted heads of white marble, as big as my fist.

One was a haunting Roman bust you'd expect to see in a museum, with a crown of thorns and a mysterious smile. The men wanted $250 U.S. for it but quickly came down to $150, even though I wasn't bartering. Then one of them hissed — "guard" — and they were gone. In the distance I saw a man approaching in a red headscarf, and I went back to ruin-watching. He ignored me, and shortly after he had passed, the statue salesmen popped up from behind another pillar. By now my wife and I had decided we didn't want to take artifacts out of Syria. It seemed wrong — and might even lead to Syrian jail, where conditions get grim reviews from Amnesty International.

For the rest of our walk we tried to ignore the hawkers who literally chased us from pillar to post, lowering their price by notches, then racing away when they spotted the guard. It was a scene from a B-movie, *Traders of the Lost Ark*.

Eventually we reached the end of the colonnade, where our driver Omar was waiting. A group of American tourists was also there with an English-speaking guide from Damascus, so I sought his advice. He said that Syrian archeological sites were poorly protected, so the coins were probably real — stolen from a grave somewhere — but the heads were more likely fake.

"If you like the head, you should buy it anyway," he added. "If it's fake no one will care, though in Syria, you never know. It might be real."

Despite his advice, we decided to leave and drove off to our second location. We hadn't gone far when we spied three motorcycles behind us and our statue-salesman-on-a-scooter pulled alongside our car, shouting: "For you, special price — only $70!" As he raced along beside us, he kept bargaining and lowering the price. Omar put his foot to the gas and left the men behind, but three kilometers on, they were waiting around a bend, having taken a shortcut. They roared alongside us again, shouting "$40 — best offer!"

The bottom was falling out of antique prices and when it hit $35, we stopped the car and gave in. Why not? At that low a price, the head was obviously an imitation, and would make a nice memento. I paid the men their money and slipped the head into my breast pocket, but just before he left, the salesman leaned into our car and said, "If anyone asks about this at the border, tell them you got it at the Damascus market. Don't say where it came from."

And so we drove away, not quite sure whether we'd bought a cheap fake, or a fantastic 2000-year-old treasure. We started to worry about what to say at the Syrian customs office: should we declare it, or hide it and hope no one saw? Was it fake or real? I'd barely owned the head and it hung over my soul like a weight.

For the next three hours we drove across the desert toward our next stop, San Simeon, an ancient church that's one of Syria's best attractions.

We arrived there late afternoon where a sleepy guard informed us the site had just closed.

We pleaded with him to let us in but he shrugged and said: "Sorry, my boss is *VERY* bad man. If he find you here, big trouble."

Omar didn't give in as easily as us. He offered the guard five dollars baksheesh and reluctantly, the man opened the gate.

"Quick! Go inside," he said, "but if trouble come, you leave quickly."

Moments later we found ourselves alone in a lovely fifth century convent, with extraordinary 30-foot stone arches lit by twilight. We spent the next ten minutes wandering through the site, then heard the guard come racing back shouting: "Someone coming — maybe boss! Must leave by back way or big trouble. Run!"

He thrust Omar's bribe back into my hands and tugged at my sleeve. Next thing we knew, we were racing after him across the church courtyard toward the other end of the site. Minutes later, we clambered over an old stone wall and found ourselves outside the church property. The guard wanted us to trek into the woods alone and meet Omar at the highway two miles away, but we said weren't bushwacking through Syria. It was a big mistake. No sooner did we round the wall than we saw a tall man dressed in black, with a Saddam Hussein-style moustache. He looked as "bad" as our guard had warned — a B-movie villain, who barked: "Where have you been!?"

Taking a walk, I said.

"No! You were *inside* San Simeon. You break law. Now you come to police station. You go to jail for a long time."

Suddenly I remembered the head — it was still in my pocket — and fear gripped me for the first time. I shivered. It was bad enough to be arrested for sneaking into Syrian ruins, but worse if they found a possibly 2000-year-old artifact on me. Either crime could be explained alone, but together they'd be enough to send us to the "Syrian Political Prison for Grave Pilferers."

I could see the headlines: "Montreal Writer Caught in Grave-Robbing Ring. Canadian Embassy Declines to Intervene."

Ahead in the parking lot, a white paddy wagon waited and I made a fast decision. As the "bad man" marched in front of me, I slipped the head from my pocket and threw it surreptitiously into the grass. If the trouble blew over, I could come back for it later.

Down in the parking lot there was a heated debate taking place in Arabic between Omar and the "bad man." The man said that he was going to get the police and ordered us to wait, then he drove away in the white wagon. Meanwhile, our guard began jabbering that the "bad man" wasn't his boss — it was another bad man he didn't know.

It was all baffling, but Omar offered some quick advice: "We must go before the man comes back." Before leaving, I ran back to find the head, but to my amazement the white rock of the statue was the generic rock of Syria: everywhere I looked I saw small lumps of white. We turned over one after another, but none had a smiling face.

As twilight turned to darkness there was nothing to do. We climbed into our car and drove off, leaving the head in the earth it had come from. Was it real or not? Worthless or priceless? The whole experience felt like a dream, but Omar was laughing.

"Statue no go to Canada" he chuckled merrily. "Statue stay home."

We joined him in laughter. In a way, we had never really owned it. The statue was staying right where it belonged, in the ruins of Syria.

THREE

City Slights

MAROONED IN MONTREAL

❖

News item: ABITIBI-PRICE AND STONE-CONSOLIDATED LTD.
TO MERGE. HEAD OFFICE TO BE LOCATED IN MONTREAL
(March 1997)

MONTREALERS ARE CHEERING the fact that Abitibi-Consolidated Ltd. will have its new headquarters here, along with several hundred jobs, the first head office to choose Montreal since John Molson started his brewery in 1782.

The big winners are the company's Montreal employees who won't have to head down the 401 to Toronto, checking their cigarettes and unpasteurized parmesan cheese at the Ontario border. But what about the losers: the dozens of nervous Toronto employees who must now move to Montreal, a city often portrayed by Ontario newspapers as the Belfast of Canada?

What do these newcomers know about their exotic new home? Can they learn to adapt? To help them out, here is a survival guide for the new Toronto refugee, exiled to Montreal.

LANGUAGE
There's no truth to the rumor you can only speak English half as loudly as French. Despite the language police, Montreal is still the only truly bilingual city in Canada, as long as you know the rules:

Rule 1: If you want to speak English in a store, just say "bone-jour" in tortured French, preferably with an American accent. Most shopkeepers will quickly switch to English to be polite and avoid listening to your French.

Rule 2: If you insist on speaking only French, that's easy too. Simply start your conversation off in loud English by saying something like "Hi there! How's it going today, eh?"

You're guaranteed to speak French for the rest of your encounter.

65

It's also wise to master new linguistic skills, such as the ability to decipher pictograms. After decades of battles over the language of signs, Quebec has found a way to avoid offending either language group, by using colorful pictograms understood by neither group.

Montreal streets are lined with mysterious pictograms that include: ??? (information kiosk), $$$ (casino), herds of white elephants (Mirabel airport) and boxes with big Xs through them (beware of explosive material) — not blockhead ahead.

If you don't have time for a Pictogram 101 course, use common sense. For instance, a picture of a car stopping for a person obviously means a red light, while a picture of a car hitting a person means a pedestrian crossing.

LIFESTYLE

Forget health food, juice bars and a diet for a small waistline; say hello to smoked meat, greasy *patates frites* and early triple-bypass surgery. When you go to a night club, Montreal bartenders expect you to order liquor—not a half-caf, decaf, low-cal latte.

And no, you can't order your poutine with low-fat cheese, balsamic vinegar, and a side order of arugula.

Montreal is the official smoking section of Canada. Quebecers smoke in bars, restaurants, schools, churches, daycare centres, and hospital emergency wards. While smoking is not yet mandatory, the non-smoking section of bars and restaurants is usually somewhere in the smoking section. In fact, you will be inhaling so much second-hand smoke, you might as well start smoking.

GETTING AROUND

In most Canadian cities you can turn right on red lights. In Montreal you can turn right on reds, or left on reds, or just go straight through a red. Stop signs are also optional, while pedestrian crossings are reserved for cars, and bus lanes are used by motorcycle gangs and police chases.

Parking is easy as long as you can understand signs that say:

Stationnement reservé détenteurs de permis de residents, secteur 33. 9h-15h; 18h-9h, sauf les fin de semaines. Livraison seulement 8h30-11h30, 1 mars-1 dec.

I don't.

SERVICES

Government offices are open 10 a.m. to noon and 2-4 p.m., though they take the phone off the hook at 2:30. If you want to go to a hospital, phone first to make sure it's still open.

If you're flying somewhere, relax, as Dorval airport is much easier to get to than Toronto's Pearson airport. However, if your flight is out of Mirabel, it's quicker to go to Dorval airport, fly to Toronto and then fly to your destination.

THINGS TO BRING

Snow removal has seen a lot of budget cuts so it's wise to bring a large shovel. It's also wise to bring your Toronto blue box: Recycling in many parts of Quebec is limited to politicians.

Don't bring that 12-foot Canadian flag you got free from Sheila Copps. Flying a block-long Maple Leaf on your front lawn may be neighborly in Toronto, but here it sends a mixed message and may result in the guy on the next balcony hauling out his 12-foot fleur-de-lis. It's safer to fly your Union Jack, since few people in Quebec know what it is.

MISCELLANEOUS

Be prepared to become a Quebec media celebrity. As a Torontonian coming to Montreal you are an oddity, somewhat like a refugee fleeing the U.S. by raft for Cuba. The media will be eager to hear your reactions. French-language TV reporters will ask if you've fallen in love with Montreal. English TV reporters will ask if you feel oppressed by French signs.

You can play it both ways since very few people watch newscasts in both languages. Consider hiring an agent and writing a book or screenplay about the experience.

Above all, remember that whatever challenges you face, you are helping to save Canada by bridging the two solitudes. Do your best to understand your new home, your new neighbors and their complex national aspirations. Then make sure you stay more than two years so you can vote No in the next referendum.

Bon voyage.
Allô police.

BULLYING THE BIKERS

❖

EVERY TIME I PICK UP THE PAPER there's another story about Montreal's biker war: a six-year battle that has seen well over 100 murders, 200 bombs, and enough drugs seized by police to pay for the federal debt. Yet despite endless police dragnets, the charges rarely stick and the motorcycle wars continue. It's time to call in reinforcements.

Let's unleash Quebec's most committed government agency, a law-enforcement agency as zealous as any on the continent. Let's sic the Quebec language police on the bikers.

Our tongue-troopers are an elite force of bureaucrats who've exhausted everyone from deli owners to tombstone makers with their raids on English language signs and menus. They've brought some of the largest corporations in the country to their knees — from Poulet Frit Kentucky (formerly Kentucky Fried Chicken) to the former Eaton (formerly Eaton's).

Yet, in recent years there are fewer and fewer English signs around to chase and more inspectors around to chase them. The language police have been reduced to harassing funeral owners whose tombstones are in Yiddish. Why not give them a job that tests their talents?

For starters, they could look into the name of our province's gangs, such as the Hell's Angels. In the last two decades we've wiped the apostrophe off everything from Bens delicatessen and Ogilvys department store to Buanderie Phils Laundry. Yet you can still see the "Hell's" apostrophe on their bikes, jackets and tattoos, not to mention every newspaper story about them. Do these guys think they're above the law?

Many other gangs are no better, from the Rock Machine and the Jokers, to the Evil Ones and the Death Riders. You can tell by their names that none of these guys have the slightest interest in promoting French. All are organizations of more than fifty people which, by law, must provide all communications in French, so why not tie them up in the paperwork that has overwhelmed other Quebec businesses?

Obviously the club name, The Hell's Angels, should be francisized to "Les Anges de l'Enfer." The rival Rock Machine gang would have to become "La Machine de Roche" and the Jokers would become "Les Blagueurs." Take that you punks — and it's just the beginning.

Look back at articles on gangs, and even francophone bikers have always had English nicknames, from Maurice "Mom" Boucher to "Snake" Tremblay, "Zig Zag" Lessard and my favourite, Philippe "Burger" Berger. Where is the *Office de la Langue Française* when you need it? Why doesn't it send these guys one of its politely worded letters laying down the language law?:

Dear Sir,

It has come to our attention that the nickname "Mom" appears on your club jacket and several of your tattoos. In itself, this is not illegal, as Quebec is, of course, one of the most democratic and tolerant societies in the world. However your nickname ("Mom") also appears frequently in the French news media in connection with alleged "club" activities, such as car bombings, fires and machine-gun executions.

We have decided this constitutes a form of personal "publicity." Therefore, we must inform you that, under article 6.4, sub-section 7(b) of the French Language Charter, any further use of the nickname "Mom" will be viewed as a commercial sign and must include a French-language version at least twice the size.

Be advised that the official translation of your name is deemed to be Maurice "La Mère" Boucher. However, other acceptable translations include: "Maman," "Mère," and "Moman" Boucher.

P.S. With regards to your fellow club member, known as Philippe "Burger" Berger, we point out that the official term for a "hamburger" in Quebec is "un hambourgeois." Therefore we advise you that Mr. Berger's nickname should be changed to the more permissible Philippe "Bourgeois" Berger.

The Hell's Angels aren't the kind of guys to roll over when attacked by a few bureaucrats, but the more they resist, the deeper they'll sink. There will be no end to the fines, summonses, injunctions and other paperwork that arrive at their clubhouse door. Inspectors will be prowling the premises every day, measuring the size of the French lettering on their *You Trespass, You Die* signs, and monitoring their club intercom to see if French is the official language of communication.

Do club officials use the correct "le vilbrequin" or the anglicized "le crankshaft?" Do they use the officially recognized term, "les bottines de ciment," or just "cement boots?"

Once the *Office* finishes harassing bikers over their names and nicknames, it can crack down on their hangouts, including those east-end strip clubs with all the flashing signs in the window saying: "Peep Show." Somehow these English words have survived for years in nightclub windows, while snack bar specials saying "Hot Chicken Sandwich" don't last a week.

Given the zeal of Quebec's language officers, the Hell's Angels and their rivals will spend much of the next five years with their lawyers, filling out forms to prove they're a cultural institution which deserves linguistic exemption. They'll be so busy meeting with bureaucrats they won't have time to make bombs.

That's how the Chicago cops finally got hold of Al Capone. They gave up trying to get him for murder and went after him for tax evasion. Let's use the same tactics here. Let's send in the GST and QST inspectors who root out the "underground economy." Do biker gangs charge GST on their drugs?

How about our Green Onion parking squad? Have you ever seen the way bikers park when they go for a steamed hot dog on the lower Main? Let's slap them with a $100 ticket, then bring in a Remorquage Québecois tow truck to haul them off to a lot in the north end of the city.

Let's throw the book at the gangs. Our bureaucrats should fine them for putting their garbage out on the wrong day, holding illegal garage sales, and forgetting to scoop up their Rottweilers' poop. Quebec's bureaucracy is a match for any gang in the world, if we give them the chance.

With a little effort, they can do for the Hell's Angels and rival gangs what they've done for so many other Quebec organizations. Imagine! — a language-police headline you would actually enjoy reading:

HEAD OFFICE LEAVING MONTREAL.
Hell's Angels Hit the 401 — for Toronto.

ALL PHONES MUST BE FRANCOPHONES

❖

News item: PQ GOVERNMENT FEARS
'RAMPANT BILINGUALISM' IN MONTREAL

Beep.

Merci d'avoir appelé le Gouvernement du Québec.
    Pour parler a une télephoniste, appuyez sur le 1.
    Pour le service automatisé en français, appuyez sur le 2.
    Pour le numéro de fax et les heures d'ouverture, appuyez sur le 3.
    For service in English, press ★32#956★0!, then wait an additional 17 seconds to annoy you and remind you this is NOT an officially bilingual service.

Beep.

You have requested English service. Please wait an extra 45 seconds on account of the PQ convention this weekend.
    The government of Quebec wishes to show that it is protecting French in Quebec—and the only way to do that is by frustrating the English. As a people, we find this slightly humiliating, but what can you do? C'est la vie.
    Please stay on the line to retain your calling priority. For rapid insta-service in French, press 1 any time.
    While you wait for the next available English-speaking operator, please listen to this pre-recorded message:

Beep.

The government of Quebec wishes to remind you that you are part of THE BEST-TREATED MINORITY IN THE WORLD, an exciting bilingual component of this great unilingual city. That's why Quebec provides extensive service in English in a variety of areas. Following are a list of them:

Beep.

You can pay all Quebec taxes — in English!
You can buy Loto-Quebec tickets — in English!
You can purchase liquor at all government outlets — in English!
Our beautiful Montreal Casino offers rampantly bilingual croupiers who will accept your money in any language you use. Book now for our special "ethnic money at par" weekend. Come on down!

Quebec also provides English-language services at selected English hospitals if you are a designated English Patient. Should your local English hospital close and you need to switch over to a French hospital, the Quebec government provides a glossary of French terms to help you communicate with unilingual medical personnel.

This will enable you to find handy French equivalents for common medical expressions like: "I have a tickle in my throat and my nose is dripping."

Or, "I have stabbing pains in the chest and I can't breathe."

Beep.

Thank you for waiting. We at the Quebec government are pleased to serve you. Please stay on the line to maintain your English-language calling priority.

There will be an additional short delay because students are demanding a tuition freeze. To show them we are generous social democrats, we are going to freeze Quebec tuition and charge twice as much for English students from the rest of Canada.

Beep.

The time is 3:15 p.m. You have reached the English operator. Because of a backlog of callers, she is very busy. You will be served in order of priority of calling. You are # 237.

Beep.

Remember, dozens of French operators are standing by to help you. Pour le service super-rapide en français, appuyez sur le 1.

Beep.

You have chosen English again. That's fine — this is your right. While waiting, you may enjoy listening to the following English recording excerpted from Premier Lucien Bouchard's famous speech at the Centaur Theatre.

Beep.

"My fellow Quebecers. The anglophone community has rights, institutions, dignity and strength that the government of Quebec will protect and preserve. When you go to a hospital, and you're in pain, you may need a blood test; but you certainly don't need a language test"— unless, of course, you live in Sherbrooke where the only English hospital has become French.

Beep.

To order a copy of Premier Bouchard's speech for $35, plus GST and QST, please press 4. Operators are standing by in both languages.

Beepbeepbeepbeepbeepbeep!

ATTENTION! ATTENTION!

There is a rampant bilingual virus reported loose in the phone system. ALL ENGLISH SYSTEMS MUST NOW CLOSE TEMPORARILY while we sweep the province of this dangerous virus!

Rampant bilingualism alert! Rampant bilingualism alert!

New emergency measures must be brought into force. They include:

● $5 million more to hire new French language inspectors.
● All bureaucrats must ask permission before they can speak publicly in English, including while on vacation in the U.S.
● Government phones must be francophones.

Zzzzzzzzzzzzzzzzzzzzzzzzzzzzzzzzzzzzzzzzzttt

Beep.

4 p.m. Sorry. False alarm.

The *Office de la Langue Française* has studied all systems and concluded the rampant bilingualism virus is stable. There has been NO increase in English whatsoever in the past year. We are sorry for the inconvenience. However, all new emergency measures remain in place anyway. Tough. We now return to our regular service.

Beep.

Congratulations! You are next. An English operator will be with you in a few moments.

Beep.

Welcome to the English office of the Quebec government! We are pleased to serve you, descendants of the conqueror. Unfortunately, it is now 4:01 p.m. Our office is closed. The office reopens Monday morning at 8:30 a.m.
Please stay on the line to maintain your calling priority.

Beep.

Our French language service remains open until 9 p.m., and all weekend.

Pour le service en français, appuyez sur le 1.

COPS AND TODDLERS

❖

In MONTREAL, you're never too young for your first brush with the law, as a two-day-old boy I know found out last week. The events leading to his first police encounter began last Wednesday night, only hours after his birth. As usual in Montreal, it was snowing...

Thursday, 1:00 a.m.

I arrive home late to find my car has been towed across the street and dumped in a snowbank, with an $80 parking ticket frozen beneath the wiper. I'm too tired to dig it out, so I leave it there overnight.

Next morning the snowbank is gone, and so is the car, towed away again. It's the beginning of a Montreal winter activity called "Quest for Car," which I know well. In fact, I am the Montreal Pasha of Parking tickets.

Friday, 11:45 a.m.

I spend the morning searching but I can't find my car. Eventually I use a pay phone to call the cops and stand freezing, as a policeman takes my license number and searches the day's towing records.

Twenty minutes later, he says there's no record of my car. He advises me to call the city's towing companies and gives me a half-dozen phone numbers to call.

Over the next hour I speak to Carlos at Remorquage Mobile towing service, Manuel at Service de Deneigement, Sylvie at Remorquage Dandurand, and Gilles at Deneigement TJR. All dutifully search their records but none has any record of my car.

I'm told the streets are jammed with towed automobiles and car-less motorists like me.

2 p.m.

Still freezing in my phone booth, I call back Steve at the police station and blow a gasket. "Where the hell is my car?" I scream.

"Y'know, I understand your frustration," replies Steve in a calm new-age tone. "I mean they tow you twice and they don't keep a record either time. I'd be pretty damn frustrated too if I were you."

Great — a police parking therapist! Next he'd be telling me that he feels my pain. Eventually, Steve gives me the phone number of the City of Montreal Traffic department. "I don't usually give out that number—but they'll know where your car is. They keep the *master list* for all towed cars."

3 p.m.

A surly city employee keeps me dangling on the line 25 minutes, as she checks the "master list."

"Sorry sir," she says when she returns. "Your car wasn't towed by anyone in the City. It must have been stolen."

"Stolen?" I repeat in disbelief. "A ten-year-old Golf with both bumpers falling off!"

"It's possible, sir," she says.

"No it's NOT possible!" I say. "Because it was stolen at exactly the same time the City of Montreal cleaned my street!"

"Don't be sarcastic, monsieur," she says icily. "Thieves often wait for the snow trucks to come to steal cars. It's an old trick... That way you don't know your car is stolen for days."

"Well," I reply through gritted teeth. "How do I get the car back from these *thieves?*"

"Call the police and report your car stolen," she says, and hangs up.

3:30 p.m.

I call back the police and report that my rusted 1990 Golf has been stolen by the City of Montreal Snow Removal department. The female police officer on duty laughs out loud but says she'll send over some officers to file a report. Where will I be for the next few hours?, she asks.

This is tricky, I explain, as I have to be somewhere rather important. The day before, my wife had given birth to our first child. Mother and son are both at the Royal Victoria Hospital maternity centre, I explain, and I should be there too.

The police officer gets very excited.

"Congratulations, monsieur!" she says. "You go right over and visit your family, and we'll contact you at the hospital."

What can I say? I take a cab to the hospital, and on the way, I tour the neighborhood again, searching one more time for my car. Twelve blocks south of our house I find it in another snowbank. This time I don't take any chances. I stop to dig it out before it's stolen again.

9:30 p.m.

I've spent the evening at the hospital with my wife and new son. I am just dressing to leave when the hospital room door open and in walks a big moustachioed cop.

"Constable Marc Favreau," he says. "I'm here about your stolen vehicle."

I tell him I called back the police five hours earlier to report the car found. He seems miffed — he's spent 20 minutes prowling the hospital looking for me. It's a perfect end to a day of perfect civic inefficiency.

Constable Favreau glowers at me, then notices the crib.

"Oh, un bébé!" he says. "What is his name?"

I explain that we haven't decided on one yet. We just call him "The Kid."

"J'aime les bébés," says Constable Favreau marching over to The Kid's crib and peeking in. "Do you think I could hold him?"

My wife and I look at each other. What can we say — he's carrying a gun. Constable Favreau reaches down into the crib and collars our son. He lifts him up and gently starts to rock him, and within minutes The Kid is sleeping in the long arms of the law.

I feel like a proud father. Over the years, I've been arrested a dozen times for everything from disturbing the peace in a Ville St. Laurent shopping centre at age fourteen, to suspected terrorism at the Israeli consulate at age thirty-five. (Innocent on both counts.)

But I didn't get picked up by the cops till I was a teenager. The Kid has gotten his start at two days old. Obviously, he's a chip off the old block.

The hospital door swings open again and my wife's obstetrician walks in. "Ohmigod!" she says, spying The Kid in the hands of an armed policeman. "Whats wrong?"

"Nothing," I say. "We're just training our child for life in Montreal."

COUNTRY FEVER

❖

I've just returned from a grueling week of deprivation for a hardened urban warrior like me. I spent a week alone in the country.

My incentive was simple. I have a writing deadline coming up and summer in the city is too distracting. There are too many cafes and street festivals, too many phone calls from friends eager to lure me outside.

I needed to unplug from the frenzy of modern life and find some solitude, and the country seemed the solution.

I have access to a small cottage in the Eastern Townships, a simple place with no TV, no CD, no stereo, radio, fax, or other electronic diversions. All it's got is an old-fashioned black rotary phone with a party line that's always got someone yakking on it. Even if friends did track me down, they'd never get through.

From the start, I knew the quiet wouldn't be easy. I am a city creature raised on smog and steamies. I would miss the hum of the traffic, but I would have the hum of the hummingbirds at the feeder out on the porch. I made a vow to spend most of the next month at the cottage — no quitting allowed.

But could I keep my word?

MONDAY: I work like a demon, because there's nothing else to do. During breaks, I take quiet walks down long dirt roads, then watch hummingbirds swarm round the feeder. Beautiful.

TUESDAY: Bored silly. I work myself into a stupor all day, then cook an elaborate dinner on the barbecue and eat it alone in three minutes. I'm finished both my novels and there is nothing to do. At night, I prowl the porch like a caged lion.

A neighbor down the road sits out on his porch for hours, staring contentedly into space. Obviously he sees something I don't. After 30 minutes, three people and a dog walk by and I get up to applaud.

TUESDAY 9 P.M.: I try to phone home in Montreal to listen to my messages, but the party line has been on the phone since I got here. I have a desperate craving for music, or a talk show, or a TV soap opera. I haven't seen a newspaper in two days — what's going on in the world? Is anyone still out there?

WEDNESDAY MORNING: I drive twenty minutes to the village for a newspaper, but the dépanneur says he's been sold out for hours. Back at the cottage, I work myself into a stupor again then take another long walk. There are wild raspberries everywhere, but I don't like raspberries.

WEDNESDAY EVENING: I sit on the porch watching the hummingbirds again and they seem less attractive all the time. The males are colorfully plumed bullies who spend life at our feeder, gobbling food. Any time a female approaches they go into a rage and chase her away. How does the species survive?

WEDNESDAY 11 P.M.: The phone rings for the first time in three days. I answer on the first ring, before the party line picks up. It's a friend calling from downtown Montreal with a gift.

"Listen," she says, and I hear a reassuring hum. "It's the sound of a late-night traffic jam."

Beautiful.

THURSDAY: Bored silly again. Some friends vacationing in the area take pity and bring me a small black-and-white TV which gets one fuzzy channel. That night it seems like a 30-inch color screen with quadrophonic sound.

FRIDAY: I wake up to write my newspaper column and the computer screen goes blank. I panic. The party line is still busy, so I drive to a nearby cottage where some friends from the city are now vacationing. They let me use their second computer for the day and casually ask how I'm doing.

When I tell them, they look amazed. How can anyone get bored in the country they ask? There's so much to do.

FRIDAY 5 P.M.: After working in their house all day, I understand their point. I also understand why so many people like the quiet of country life. Their cottage is filled with color TVs, VCRs, a CD player, cappuccino-maker, stereo, shortwave radio, electronic bread-maker, electric barbecue and other toys. All that's missing is a Ferris wheel.

How can they find time to be bored?

FRIDAY NIGHT: I'm back in Montreal briefly to stock up on emergency items: shortwave radio, tape deck, halogen lamps, case of wine and cordless push-button phone. I'm still looking for a portable color TV. I've discovered a giant antenna on the cottage roof and if I connect it, I can get CNN and maybe even Star TV from India.

I am also making plans to hire a comedy team from Yuk Yuks to come out Wednesday and entertain on my porch. Thursday I am throwing a Festival of the Barbecue. I have decided country living is fine, as long as you bring along the city.

PAS D'ENGLISH

❖

To your battle posts, anglos!
Alliance Quebec leaders here in Montreal want us to boycott all businesses that don't have English-language signs, including the Royal Bank, Canadian Tire and several restaurants that refuse to post the English word "pouteen."

More English signs around town certainly wouldn't hurt anyone, but I'm not sure a boycott is the best way to get results. Our community no longer has enough buying power for stores to notice.

I have a better plan, a strategy to bring every French-only business in Quebec to its knees overnight, including the Quebec government. It is time to unleash the one real power that remains to our anglophone community: The A-bomb of the language war — our bad French.

We must boycott English. As Quebecers, we have the right to insist on being served in French only, no matter how bad our French is. If we use this right effectively, we can bring Quebec business to a standstill.

How would my plan work? It's simple ...

Almost two-thirds of anglophones and allophones now speak French fluently, including everyone under thirty. But many of the remaining third still can't speak much French at all. They are usually older anglos, raised in the days when French schools wouldn't accept them and English schools wouldn't teach them French.

A relative of mine is typical — I'll call her Aunt Ida. Ida never learned French and today she is still too embarrassed to speak it much in public. She says a hearty "bone-jour," and hopes the store clerk will be kind enough to switch to English. But if Ida and her ilk ever insisted on speaking French in stores, the result would be devastating.

So why waste time with a shopping boycott that may produce little but tension? Let's send in Ida and a squad of unilingual anglos and bring these stores to their knees. Imagine the scene at Provigo's food counter:

AUNT IDA: Bone-jour! Je vous acheter le — uh — comment dites ça — uh — le jam-bone. C'est fresse?

SALESMAN: Je m'excuse madame. Qu'est-ce-que vous voulez exactement? I think you mentioned le jambon? Do you want some ham?

IDA: Oui, may juste du petit tronch—ne pas très meggre, may ne pas très grand. Je vouler...uh..un quartier de livre — quatruh-onze — et..uh...tronchez comme demi-pousse. Very fresse — pas old.

SALESMAN: Desolé, madame. I do not really understand you. Maybe you should speak English? I know a lit-tle...

IDA: Non! Je ne vouler pas en anglais. ... Je insist que jay, uhh... le droit pour parler Français!

SALESMAN: Bon, madame. I will try to go slowly. Je — vais — parler — lentement. Quel — sorte — de — jambon — voulez — vous?

IDA: Pardon? Je ne comprenner pas.

SALESMAN: Madame! I cannot spend all day here with you. There are many customers waiting! Could you please speak English? Please?

IDA: Non! Et mon *non* ay Québecois!

Face it, a dozen Idas could tie up Provigo for days, as well as any other store that didn't give in. Within a week, there'd be big English signs popping up in every business that serves anglophones. Then we could send Ida down to deal with government offices, like the license bureau, where language minister Louise Beaudoin has instructed her bureaucrats to give things an all-French look.

IDA: Bone-jour! Je vous information pour — uh — automobile.

CIVIL SERVANT: Oui, madame. Voulez-vous la nouvelle immatriculation ou une plaque?

IDA: Plaque? What do you mean my teeth have plaque!? Quel insulte! Say très humiliation pour moi. Je demand un apology!

CIVIL SERVANT: Excusez-moi, madam, I'm not a dentist! I meant your "plaque d'automobile." Your license plate. Do you want a new license plate, or something else?

IDA: Pas d'English! Je suis Québecois! Say ma droit pour parler en francais quand je vouler. Si vous parler anglais, je telephone la langue police maintenant!

CIVIL SERVANT: Madam. I am only trying to help you understand

IDA: Français! Français! Au secours! Mes droits! Madame Beaudoin!!!

Once Ida and her gang have dealt with the small fish, we can move the English boycott to larger prey, like Bell Telephone. In fact if your French is bad enough, you can help out from home.

Just phone up the operator, push 1 for French, and then refuse to speak a word of English to her, no matter how frustrated they get. If you get cut off, call up the language police and report that the operator refused to serve you in French. Anonymously, of course. Under Bill 101, this is your right.

You can also use the English boycott in the next referendum vote too, to make sure the question is perfectly clear. Just insist on your right to answer the French version of the question.

The more confusing it is, the longer you'll stand in the voting booth trying to figure out what the question means. As voting starts to drag over several days, the government will be forced to switch to a simpler question everyone can understand:

INDÉPENDANCE
–Oui?
–Non?

Take my advice, English-speaking Montrealers. The only power left to you is the power to speak French badly. Use it or lose it. Come next April, insist on filling out your income-tax form in French.

Then send in a half-filled out form, with a note saying: "Je ne comprenner pas et je ne payer pas. Mercy."

MOONSHINE MUSEUM

❖

QUEBEC'S PLAN TO CREATE a new $8 million Museum of Alcohol is a lush and spirited idea, which deserves a toast. It's the latest brainchild of the Quebec Liquor Board which hopes to attract tourists as well as visiting high school classes to show them how beer, scotch, and rye are made.

Presumably there will also be a local wine-making exhibit to show how grape concentrate from France is mixed with water at the Montreal port to create Château Dépanneur. Also useful would be interactive exhibits like a beat-the-breathalyzer test, to answer the question:

How Drunk Can You Drive?

Some governments might shy away from a shrine to moonshine but it seems in character with Quebec. Our province already has 460 museums, but the Museum of Booze shows we've only scratched the surface of many unique Quebec activities that deserve their own museums. How about opening a:

MUSEUM OF STRIKES

For decades we led North America with our yearly line-up of police, fire, blue collar, nurses, doctors, ambulance, seaway, transit and common front strikes. Exhibits could include things like a bus vandalized during the great transit strike and a bombed-out taxi from the night the Murray Hill strike met the Montreal police strike.

The only problem this museum would face would be embarassment when the staff walked out demanding higher pay.

MUSEUM OF SIGNS

We have the material for a world-class museum unlike any on earth.

In the last twenty years, Quebecers have created some of the most creative signs in the world — like Ye Aulde Curiousté Shoppe, which mixed French and old English to try and get around the language law.

Isn't it time we showed off our achievements to the world? Think of the fascinating exhibits we could mount.

- The Missing Apostrophe Room: (Including the original

apostrophes from Eatons, Murrays, Mckennas, Pascals, Steinbergs, Irvs Place and thousands of other signs that had them removed.

- Informers' Alley: The original letters and e-mail from all the anonymous people who've sent in complaints fingering English signs. "C'est affreux. Il y a une affiche illegale qui dit 'URGENCE/EMER-GENCY" sur un hôpital près de ma maison....C'est too much.'"
- Interactive: An official OLF tape measure would let you be the language inspector: You could measure the lettering on everything from matzoh boxes and Chinese menus to tombstones to see if you spot the illegal English sign.

There could also be quizzes like:

Which of the following signs is illegal?

1–VIDEO MOVIELAND.
2– EGGSPECTATION
3– BOUTIQUE BLUESONTHEGREEN.
4– STOP/ARRET
(★answer at end of story)

THE MUSEUM OF VOLONTARY TAXES

A shrine to ex-Mayor Jean Drapeau, who created Canada's first lottery to pay for the Olympic deficit, and showed politcians everywhere that you can always soak a citizen for more. Quebec has stayed ahead of the other provinces with creative use of video terminals, lotteries, bingo games, and casinos that make us the one-armed bandit of fleecing ourselves.

Museum exhibits could include famous dépanneurs who've sold winning tickets, famous lawsuits between families who went to court over the money, and interviews with some of the millions of losers who've sold off cars and RRSPs to play the odds against their government.

To pay for itself, the museum would also double as a casino where you could play all the exhibits. Be warned, the house always wins — and you can lose your house.

THE MUSEUM OF SEPARATISM

Lets take take a tip from Cuba's Museum of the Revolution, a huge dusty place where they display everything from old tanks and guns to Che's clothing and Fidel's cigars. Imagine our own Museum of Independence!

Artifacts could include:

–A roomful of spoiled West End ballots.
–A huge carton of head offices.
–Claude Ryan's Beige Paper on Independence.
–René Lévesque's rolling paper.
–An ethnic and some money.

There could also be a special exhibit of the anglo "brain drain." Given all the talented people who have been educated by Quebec and left, why not ask them to send their brains back for display once they're finished with them?

There could even be a special interactive Question Room where a a computer would help you create your own tricky referendum question — then test it against a sample group of Quebecers to see if it gets a YES answer.

For instance: "Do you NOT disagree that Quebec should NOT become a sovereign country in the event that it does or does not get a NO from Canada in proposed negotiations with the government of Quebec NOT?"

The Museum of Separatism would be designed in a circular revolving shape so that when you arrived at the end, you'd have to start all over at the beginning again.

MUSEUM OF CONSTRUCTION
A perfect use for the Big O, which is still under construction 23 years later.

MUSEUM OF BUREAUCRACY
Open holiday Mondays only, except during coffee break and lunch, and during sick days. Phone before coming to confirm we are open.

(★The illegal sign is #4. All of the others have been around for years in Montreal.)

ICE STORM SURVIVOR GUILT

❖

THREE WEEKS AFTER THE ICE STORM of the Century, Montreal is divided into two groups of people: those who feel they've suffered terribly, and those who feel they haven't suffered enough.

So far, we've heard a lot from the sufferers: how they lived without heat, light, hot water and Pulse News. This week, we're hearing about how they're still suffering, from something called "post-storm acute traumatic stress."

The symptoms include nightmares, flashbacks, insomnia, claustrophobia and I-got-no-plumberophobia.

But the other group has been ignored completely and it's time someone showed us some sympathy. Like me, many Montrealers were away on holiday during the big storm and only returned afterwards. We too are suffering from a little-discussed condition, called Post Ice Guilt Syndrome: PIGS.

Some of you envy us, but you don't understand our distress.

When the storm hit I was in Havana, working. The first I heard about it was when I casually passed a hotel television that was broadcasting CNN. They were featuring a news report about a freak ice storm somewhere in North America, where crushed power pylons, toppled trees and a grim arctic landscape looked like a scene from Outer Irkutskaya, Siberia.

As I looked more closely at the reporter beneath the parka, I saw the familiar face of CBC's Mark Kelley, and heard myself groan. "Oh God — it's Montreal!"

Soon after, I was on the phone talking with family and friends, listening to their problems. My house still had power but my wife's parents had been forced to move in with us. My sister-in-law was huddled over a wood stove in NDG and my brother-in-law was moving from house to house like a nomad.

My friends were scattered about the city like refugees and one had had his car sliced in half by a falling tree. Another had sixteen people living at his house and a third spent days by her living room fireplace, dreaming of the luxury of a hot meal. I hung up the phone and rushed off to share the bad news with some Cuban friends. As I described what had happened, they became very concerned.

"It sounds terrible!" said one man. "How many people are dead?"

"Well — only a few so far," I answered "but a million people have no heat or electricity."

"Oh, that is very difficult," said the Cuban, obviously unimpressed. "Have many of the buildings in Montreal collapsed?"

"Uh, no, they're too well-built for that," I said. "But my in-laws have had to move in with us."

"That must be hard", sympathized another man in his thirties. "I live with my mother and brother and it's not easy sharing one room."

"Well, actually," I said, "We have...seven rooms."

During the rest of my stay in Cuba I talked regularly to Montreal by phone but stopped trying to explain things to Cubans. To them our first-world emergencies are the problems of everyday life, while their catastrophes usually involve large funerals.

Since arriving back home this week, I've found myself seeing things through Cuban eyes as well as my own. I've done my best to feel the city's pain, but I'm like a Londoner who returned home after the Blitz. I haven't changed, but Montreal has. Every gathering I go to now starts with the same greeting:

"Hi! How long was it for *you*?" Then, everyone starts trading stories like old soldiers at a Legion Hall.

"No power for five days? That's nothing! We had no power for a week — and the last two days we survived on cold Campbell's chicken soup and processed white bread!"

Meanwhile we people with PIGS sit quietly in the corner afraid to open our mouths. Some old friends who endured the ice storm have turned into Montana-style survivalists, and I can hardly communicate with them. If a lightbulb burns out in the living room, they leap up in panic shouting: "Ohmigod! It's the main frame generator in James Bay! Get the kids to the fireplace!"

They wander around their house in bike helmets and keep stacks of candles on every table, along with five litres of water and an emergency supply of tea biscuits. They've got a priority list of which furniture they can burn first.

"We're not out of the woods yet," they keep telling me. "Things may *look* normal but believe me, we're only one wire away from the Flintstones."

They won't let their kids play in the park, which they believe is more dangerous than a mine shaft.

"William, get away from those trees right now!" they shout at their ten-year old. "Be a good boy and go play in the traffic!"

Meanwhile those of us with PIGS are alone and alienated, destined to re-live forever what we never lived, because no one will discuss anything else. My own paper, the Montreal *Gazette*, has become a kind of Ice Journal, filled with 1001 stories of the storm. Thank God for Bill Clinton's extra-marital affairs; at last there's been something else to read.

I know that I must try harder to understand. I know that people are still living in darkness and I am one of the lucky ones. I know that my credibility as a columnist is ruined. I am supposed to be some kind of Montreal weathervane, and I missed the weather event of the century.

When the temperature got cold last week I casually mentioned to someone that it was "pretty miserable" outside.

"Miserable? What do you know about miserable?" she snapped. "How dare you talk about the weather, when you weren't here for IT!...You'll never understand Montreal again."

OK, I get the message, but what should us storm-dodgers do now that we've missed the draft? How many front walks must we shovel, how many cars must we dig out before we are pardoned?

Should we turn off our power for a week and live in the dark, boiling our water? Should we lock ourselves in a meat cooler and heat by charcoal broiler until we asphyxiate? Maybe we could just do something symbolic — like spend a week at the Ice Capades in our jockey shorts?

Several people I know with PIGS are talking about forming a support group that could sit in the dark, trade stories and listen to tapes with testimonials by ice storm survivors. In the meantime, I hear they're selling T-shirts saying: "I survived the Great Ice Storm."

How about a T-shirt for those of us who didn't? It could say:

Sorry I missed the Great Ice Storm.
Please tell me your story. Again.

FOUR

Health Scare

MY NOSE KNOWS NOT

❖

AHH, THE SWEET SMELLS OF SUMMER: flowers in bloom, fresh hay, the pungent scent of milkweed wafting across the — ah, why pretend? The truth is I can't smell a rose unless it's stuck in my nose. I can barely smell the difference between a lilac and an old sock. I am nasally-challenged, part of an overlooked minority group that gets little attention.

If you read my stories you will see lots about Montreal sights, sounds, tastes and feelings. But there's rarely a scent to be found, because I rarely smell them. Oh sure, I can smell a dead fish if you stick it in my face, or freshly ground coffee if my nose is inside the bag. But I have to be so close to whatever I'm inhaling that I'm not really smelling it. I'm tasting it.

To look at my nose, it's quite an impressive appendage, but bigger is not necessarily better when it comes to smelling. My schnoz is really just an ornament, a large decorative object good for little but holding up sunglasses. It breathes, it sneezes and it freezes in winter — but left to its own devices, it couldn't track down a skunk.

I have met others like me, a silent minority of nasal nobodies who dare not speak their shame. You see them everywhere, standing around quietly while some olfactory show-off shouts: "God, smell those lilies. Makes you feel alive, doesn't it?"

No one cares about our plight. Look around and you'll see support groups for the vertically-challenged and the horizontally-challenged; for the toothless, the sightless, the childless, the parentless and the penniless—but not for the scentless. There are no charities for the nasally-deprived, with appealing names like "Cents for scents." Too bad, because I could be their poster boy.

Like many of the nasally-challenged I live vicariously, building a fantasy life based on other people's aromas. I read novels with a thousand smells and try to imagine them — like Byron's "sweet smell of bread and butter" — though I'm not sure whether he meant one smell or two.

I remember *Perfume*, a novel about a murderer with such a refined sense of smell he would track down his victims by their scent. But like most perfume, it was wasted on me. Humans are supposedly able to discern 10,000 odours, but I got shortchanged. How did I come to be such a nasal nerd?

As a child I had sinus problems, and doctors prescribed every drug on the shelves to help me breathe. I took Contac C and Coricidin D, huge sinus tablets and tiny time capsules. I was a toxic dump for nose drops: the Love Canal of the nasal world. Like an addict who needs ever-bigger fixes, I upped my doses all the time, until eventually I must have damaged my sniffer's sensitivity. I was a victim of sinus substance abuse.

Sometimes I think I should do TV ads warning what happens when you OD on nose drops, but that would be too negative. I'd prefer to think of myself as a success story — proof that in the modern urban world, you can survive without smells.

Unlike my caveman ancestors, I don't have to sniff out my food; I can ask for it at the grocery, or order it from a take-out restaurant. I don't have any predators to sniff out either, unless you count a speeding SUV, which you can hear long before you smell it. I don't need my nose to smell sour milk or rotten eggs — I just read the expiry date — and when it comes to detecting smoke, I buy lots of fire alarms.

There might even be some advantages to being nasally-disadvantaged. I miss out on what I'm told are a lot of vile smells, from diesel fumes to bad breath. When I drive to the country and pass our local pig farm, everyone on the highway holds their nose except me. In a financial pinch, I could probably raise pigs.

I know a sense of smell enhances the joy of eating, but a hearty appetite has never been my problem, as anyone who has seen me eat can attest. I have enough taste buds in my mouth to compensate for my lack of smell. Or maybe I have a phantom palate.

Ultimately, I like to think that I am not really nasally-disadvantaged at all. I am nasally-evolved, a triumph of natural selection, an evolutionary leap forward toward an exciting new species that does not need a nose to survive.

Call me post-nasal man.

ONCE UPON A MATTRESS

❖

I HAVE ALWAYS BEEN somewhat fussy about beds. As a lifetime insomniac, I've learned that a lumpy hotel mattress can keep me awake all night, like a princess sleeping on a pea.

I'm also a restless sleeper, so my bad night's sleep can quickly become my wife's. That's why we recently decided to get a better bed, something soft enough for me to sink into but firm enough to keep her afloat. It seemed a simple matter until we stepped into our first mattress store.

We quickly discovered that there are more models of mattress than stars in the galaxy. Like cars, they come in a bewildering array of options: in singles, doubles, queens, kings and twins, with or without pillow-top padding, in plushly firm, extra-firm, medium-firm and medium-fat — hold the mustard.

The Big 3 mattress-makers — Simmons, Sealy, and Serta — each feature hundreds of different models, with minute differences and immense price differences. They go by names like the Prestige, the Connoisseur, the Divine, the Sublime, the Intimate and the Exquisite, and figuring out the difference between them is the Headache.

To start with, a bed isn't easy to test. Walk into your average mattress store and most people are wandering about shyly poking and prodding the product, as if they were looking for something to insulate their homes. But a bed is made to sleep in, and the only reliable test is to lie down on the job. It's a bit embarrassing at first, but you get used to it.

On entering a mattress shop, my wife and I would immediately plop down on the first comfortable-looking bed we saw, with our shoes dangling off the edge. Then I'd roll around a bit and turn over violently.

"Move around more," she'd say. "That's not how you toss at night. Thrash your arm like you do at 4 a.m."

Then I'd toss and turn some more as the customers stared at us in shock. It's a sensitive business and it helps to have a trustworthy salesperson — but most mattress-sellers give used-car salesmen a good name.

Mattresses range from $400 to $4,000 and you need to comparison shop. But the bed business discourages this so much they put up signs saying NO SHOPLIFTING OR COMPARING PRICES WITH OUR COMPETITORS.

Many stores promise to match any price you find for the same bed. But they neglect to mention that you won't find the same-name bed in another store, because it doesn't exist. Each store carries its beds under its own special model, with their own special colours, names and prices.

At one popular Montreal chain we found a bed we liked called the *World Class Ultra Alliance*. But we didn't like the price — $500 more than an apparently identical bed we'd seen in a small store a week earlier. The small store claimed it was exactly the same bed by the same company — only it was called the *World Class Ultra 'Regent'*. So we asked the manager of the big store if there was a difference.

"I couldn't really say," she sniffed. "We don't carry the other bed."

"But they're both World Class Ultra beds made by the same manufacturer, with the same specifications and the same materials, I said. "How big can the difference be?"

"They could be very similar, sir — but who knows? For example, why don't you try that bed over there?" She pointed to yet another identical bed by the same company, with yet another name. I lied down, and it was so hard they could have sold it to monks in a Tibetan monastery, with a name like the "Exquisite Ascetic."

"This is awful," I said, leaping up.

"You see, sir. Every bed is slightly different and you've got to be careful where and who you buy it from."

Looking back, I believe the bed she showed me wasn't actually meant to sleep in: it was a prop filled with bricks designed to frighten anyone trying to comparison shop — and it worked. By the time I left the store, I was ready to give up and sleep on the floor.

My wife, a hardened journalist, decided to get to the bottom of things. She called Simmons, the manufacturer of both beds, and asked the representative if there was any difference. The woman reacted as if she'd been asked for the formula to the atom bomb.

"Oh, we can't tell you that," she said. "That's top-secret. Mattress stores are very competitive and we never discuss the differences between our models."

Frankly, we still don't know if the beds we saw are similar or completely different. No one would tell us. The bed business awaits a Ralph Nader to roll back the blanket of deception and reveal what's under the covers.

In the end, we managed to find a reasonably inexpensive bed that we tried out and ordered, and we sleep a lot better than we used to. But I won't tell you what we bought. When it comes to beds I've learned to trust no one, including me.

It's probably best to buy *and* make your own bed. If you're lucky, you'll get to sleep in it.

WHAT, MEN WORRY?

❖

ACCORDING TO A RECENT STUDY, women find life more hazardous to their health than men do. A Health Canada survey asked people how they felt about 38 potentially dangerous areas of life, and women saw far more danger in 37 of them.

64% of women thought sunbathing was highly risky, compared to only 41% of men. Women also worried more about AIDS, crime, car accidents, ozone depletion, pesticides, alcohol consumption, food additives, tap water and mercury in their dental fillings.

They even worried about food irradiation, while very few men knew what it was. What's up? To you women, the world is a highly dangerous place; a daily tightrope walk to get back to the safety of bed. To us men, the world is just a big trampoline. Why do you women find the world so scary? Are you completely paranoid, or just realistic? Or are you just biological nurturers, programmed to worry for all of us?

In my family, my mom was also the designated worrier. She worried about how warmly we dressed and how much we ate. She worried about car accidents, kidnappings and the constant danger that I would get electrocuted while listening to the battery-powered transistor radio in the bathtub.

But when something actually did go wrong, all the men in the family panicked and my mother was strangely calm. She had spent so much time worrying about what might go wrong that she was ready for anything when it happened.

"Stop crying honey...You'll be OK. You just got a bad shock because you took your transistor radio into the bathtub."

Like my mother, many women do a lot of "anticipatory worrying" — thinking about all the things that *could* happen. Meanwhile, men never worry about anything until it happens. They live in complete denial until there's a real problem, then they panic. A woman will tell a man 4,000 times to wear sunscreen and stay out of the sun. But he will calmly brush her off.

"Stop being paranoid, honey. It's just a little sun."

But if the same man sees a tiny mark on his arm, he will instantly change his thinking.

Man: Ohmigod it's skin cancer, or leprosy! Quick honey — call an ambulance!

Woman: Relax, dear, it's a ketchup stain from your sandwich.

The truth is that many of us men move through life like a dog trotting through a minefield. When something does go wrong, we react by getting all excited and taking charge, to cover up the fact we have absolutely no idea what to do.

Men do worry about some things more than women do, but they're not the kind of things a survey would ask. For instance, if you asked Montrealers if they worry very much about the danger the Canadiens won't make the Stanley Cup playoffs this year, the results would probably be:

Men: 78%

Women: 0.0002%

Men also do a lot more worrying about why women look worried. "Uh-oh, she looks upset. Is she worried about ozone depletion and food irradiation? Or did I forget to take out the garbage?"

Women might not know it, but we men are nowhere near as cool and collected as we try to appear. Many of us spend hours agonizing over life's small risks, but unlike women, we do it when everyone else is asleep.

We race through our days, forgetting to worry about anything. Then, at 4 a.m., we wake up and think of all the things we forgot to worry about. We worry about work and about vacation. We worry about whether we turned off the stove, parked the car on the right side of the street or left our wallet on the subway seat.

If we lie awake long enough, we can start to worry about anything. In fact, if Health Canada did the same survey at 4 a.m., I suspect most men would say they worried about sunbathing, AIDS, crime, car accidents, ozone depletion, pesticides, alcohol consumption, food additives, tap water, and mercury in their dental fillings.

Meanwhile women would say that very few of the activities mentioned seemed dangerous at that moment, because they had exhausted themselves worrying about them all day.

After the pollster had left, men would lay awake thinking about all the new things the poll had given them to worry about—like food irradiation. Women would fall back to sleep instantly, murmuring to their mates: "Get some rest, dear, there's a lot to worry about in the morning."

GAS AND BYPASS

❖

FINALLY THERE'S SOME GOOD NEWS for Canadian shoppers who can't find anything worth buying in the States. Cross-border shopping may be dead, but cross border medicine is coming our way, offering new consumer thrills.

A medical centre in Plattsburgh, N.Y. is creating an array of new health services aimed at Canadians tired of lining up at their own hospitals. The centre will offer us everything from insta-cataract surgery ($850 Can.) to hip replacements and diagnostic colonoscopies ($600), as well as a new treatment for prostate cancer not yet available in Canada ($10,000).

Goodbye factory outlet, hello medical outlet. How long can it be before we see big-box stores near the border named Heart Depot, Ikneea and Prostates 'R' Us? Not to mention billboard ads, like the ones that used to advertise duty-free liquor.

- COME TO CATARACT CITY. BRIGHTEN UP YOUR DAY!
- DOUBLE DISCOUNT HIP REPLACEMENTS. Prices slashed! All hips must go.
- GAS AND BYPASS: Fillerup!

As our own medical system continues to deteriorate, more and more Canadians will spend their weekends browsing the windows at the medical mall:

"Look, honey, there's a sale on appendectomies — only $500 for two! Why don't we both get ours out now, the waiting line will be endless if we ever need one in Canada?"

Plattsburgh's new facilities will be in a former strip mall just off Interstate 87, where Canadians used to buy cheap sneakers when our dollar was worth something. But now it will be a medi-mall, small storefront specialty clinics offering everything from ultrasound tests to brain-tumour therapy. You can be sure these clinics will have catchy American names like "Xtra-fast X-rays," "Kidney Korner" and "Drive-in Dialysis."

Critics complain that, unlike our medicare system, some Canadians won't be able to afford treatment. But I'm sure American medical entrepreneurs will find ways to offer services for almost every Canadian budget:

American Plan: Includes room, spa, gourmet menu, golf, pool, prep, surgery, and bypass. Complimentary physiotherapy with five-year guarantee on all parts and labor. Only $23,999!

Canadian Plan: Includes double heart bypass, (one per patient) for shared room. Tasty sandwiches. BYOBed. All parts reliable factory seconds, with three-month guarantee. Only $6,999 Canadian.

Maternity Specials: We deliver your baby: $3,000. U-Deliver your own baby. Only $299. For a limited time only: twins at half price. Have one, get one free!

As word of the new medi-mall spreads, Quebecers will be pouring into the States again, but instead of smuggling out polo shirts in our trunk, we'll be smuggling out heart valves in our chests. As the volume grows, expect the Canadian government to start looking for GST and other taxes, by posting a medical customs officer at the border:

Anything to declare, sir?
No. I just went over for some some medical treatment. I got a new pacemaker.
Do you have a receipt for that, sir?
Uh, no, but it only cost $100. It was on special, reduced from $1,500.
Sorry, sir, I'm going to have to charge you full-price duty on that, unless you can find the receipt. Now would you mind stepping inside for a medical exam so we can see if you've purchased any other new body parts.?'

There may be other downsides to speedy medical services offered by doctors eager to make a buck, in a country where surgeons average $500,000 U.S. a year. Recent statistics show as many as 98,000 Americans die each year from medical mistakes, and you have to wonder if some of these incidents aren't related to a rush for profit.

Still, more and more Canadians are ready to risk U.S. fast-food medicine rather than wait forever for Canadian medicare. So before you get stuck in a year-long lineup at your hospital, perhaps it's time to act preventatively. Look for those new signs on the highway:

Early Bird Special: Beat the crowds. Replace aging body parts before they break down with the ALL U-CAN-TREAT BUFFET MEDICAL SPECIAL! For a simple, no-frills fee of $250,000 you get all the work you'll ever need — done now!

Have your appendix out. Replace worn knees, tired corneas and other aging parts. Remove a few ribs, before you crack one in old age and have to spend years waiting for surgery.★

★ WARNING: This offer is not available to U.S. citizens, because of federal restrictions on dangerous surgery that do not apply to foreign visitors. Canadians welcome!

EYES WIDE SHUT

❖

The problem started a few months ago, when Campbell's soup started printing the ingredients on their tins in smaller lettering. This was around the same time that pill bottles started shrinking their print too, along with a conspiracy of other products such as menus, paperbacks, and highway signs. Was there a print shortage?

The big clue came when I couldn't make out someone waving at me from below my balcony and shouting my name.

"Who is it?" I asked, peering at the strange face two floors down.

"It's me — your brother!" came the irritated reply.

Hmmm. Maybe it was time to see an eye doctor, not that there was anything wrong with my eyes. I've always thought of myself as Eagle-eye Freed, a guy who can see a country mile, even in the city. I can spot a parking spot from a block away, then get to it across three lanes of speeding traffic while reading the no-parking signs and watching for cops in my rear view mirror.

I figured my good vision was just fair compensation for the fact I have no sense of smell, I don't hear that well, and I began to lose my hair shortly after I grew it. But I figured wrong.

In the past few months my eagle-eyes have been declining so rapidly that my nearest winged equivalent may soon be the bat. I have trouble seeing highway exits until I've passed them, I can't read parking signs (or parking tickets), and I have to pore over instructions on packaged foods to find out it just says "BOIL."

A couple of months ago, I reluctantly called an opthamologist I know. He was leaving for a month's holiday and offered to refer me to someone else, but I told him it wasn't urgent and I'd see him whenever he got back.

Not that I was trying to delay getting glasses, mind you, as several of my friends had done out of vanity. One had procrastinated for so long he could barely identify which of his kids he was talking to, as he insistently told her his vision was fine.

I'd never do that, I told myself. I didn't really mind the idea of wearing glasses — I'd get them as soon as I really had to — but what was the rush? I could wait a month or two, or whatever...

Within a week of the opthamologist's departure, my eyesight sank another small but critical notch. I couldn't quite read the subtitles at a movie one night, and my companion had to explain the plot to me like I was three.

Out on the street, people thought I was being rude because I didn't recognize them until they'd practically passed by. One strange woman started staring at me outside the St. Lawrence bakery, then followed me inside and glared at me some more from across the room. Finally she came over to confront me.

"Suzanne?" I said, as her face suddenly came into focus.

"No, the Duchess of Windsor," she snapped, none too happy at being ignored.

My sight was becoming so poor that I borrowed a friend's glasses, which improved my vision somewhat. Unfortunately, my friend is a woman, and her glasses made me look like a drag queen wannabe, but I didn't care.

After months of ignoring my fading sight I was beginning to get panicky, as my inner hypochondriac went to work. My eyesight seemed to be getting worse by the day, and I wondered what would happen if it kept on declining. How would I write without vision? Why had I never learned to touch-type?

By the time my eye doctor returned to town, I had gone from denial to near-obsession. He put me through a battery of tests and announced that my eyes had no serious problem. I was just very near-sighted and wearing someone else's glasses.

He fiddled with some lenses, handed me the strength I needed — and suddenly the world came into focus like one of those Kodak ads that promise you photos "more real than life." Everything seemed clearer and more colorful than I remembered it being for years. I was living in IMAX!

The next day I went out and bought my first pair of glasses and I have to say it's amazing to see all the things I haven't seen for ages. I can see bugs scurrying about the sidewalk and small architectural details on the top of old buildings. I even have a new, high-definition television, although I still have the same old TV.

I guess Eagle-eye Freed had been deluding himself for a few years, adapting to eyesight that was fading so gradually he hadn't noticed. The only reason I thought I had good vision was that I had forgotten what it was like to see well.

Looking in the mirror, I'm still not quite accustomed to the guy in the wire-frame glasses staring back at me, but at least I can see him. And when I walk in the street, I recognize everyone I know.

They just don't recognize me.

WHINING AND DINING

❖

I'VE JUST RETURNED from the quintessential American voyage: a trip down the U.S. fast food highway.

According to recent news stories, dining while driving is the latest rage in the battle to cut the time needed to eat. A quarter of American meals are eaten in fast food chains, and now one in ten is being eaten *in* the car. It's called "dashboard dining"—and McDonald's food innovators are already inventing special dishes like the McSalad-Shaker, served in a plastic cup that fits into your cup holder.

As always, your roving gourmet is on the cusp of the new movement. I've often grabbed a café au lait and croissant to go, but on my recent U.S. trip, I ate a dozen consecutive fast food meals, mostly while driving. Here is the diary of a POFFL — a Prisoner of the Fast Food Lane.

DAY 1: 10 a.m: I fly to the American mid-west to work on a documentary film about people who chase tornadoes. I get an airline "breakfast" of pretzels and chocolate chip cookies — and my lunch is a processed cheese and ham wrap. Little do I know it's the best food I will see that week.

3 p.m: We land in Denver, and start a 300-mile drive east to meet our storm chasers. We figure we'll catch a good dinner along the way, but this isn't Quebec. The U.S. Midwest is a desert of decent food at the best of times and it's Memorial Day weekend.

For 150 miles every restaurant en route is closed. At 9 p.m. we finally pull into the small town of Brush, Colorado where 100 motorists are lined up at what's obviously the only open restaurant in the state — Wendy's.

We wait in line 50 minutes to order our "fast" food. When I get to the counter I'm so hungry I order like a prisoner on death row: one "Big Bacon Classicburger" (580 calories), a "Biggie Fries"(570 cals), a Caesar salad with ranch dressing (560 cals), and a "chocolate frosty dairy dessert" drink (540 cals) so thick you need a suction pump to drink it.

According to Wendy's nutritional guide my total intake is 2620 calories — the recommended JUNK FOOD limit for three days.

DAY 2: At 7 a.m. I catch up with my storm-chasers, who outline their schedule. They drive 14 hours a day chasing cloud formations, and waste no time stopping to eat. They are committed dashboard diners who "grab" food on the run — and if we want to film them, we have to keep up.

We start our gourmet tour by gulping down a motel breakfast of fruit loops and white bread, then hit the highway, munching on nachos from the motel dispensing machine. We spend the day driving through Nebraska and Kansas, on small backroads where restaurants are as common as ski hills.

The closest thing to a grocery is a gas station "convenience store," with endless rows of chocolate bars, Pringles, and cheese popcorn. It's known as Road Food and I stock up on the healthiest stuff I can find — big packs of cashews coated with enough salt to protect a Canadian driveway all winter.

3 p.m.: We spot our first restaurant, a take-out chicken counter. The glutinous deep fried chicken'n'fries deposited in our styrofoam boxes make Colonel Sanders look like lean cuisine. On the plus side, I discover it's easy to eat a drumstick while you're driving, McDonald's food innovators take note.

5 p.m.: We've now crossed over what I call the "creamer line," into a region of the midwest where coffee is rarely served with milk — just powdered creamer. We keep enormous cups of creamered coffee on the dashbard to wash down all the cashews.

9 p.m.: After a 14-hour driving day, we pull into a one-restaurant town — at Hardee's. It offers a wide selection of deep-fried food, with signs saying "Go LARGE with Big Fries." It's honest advertising: the people in line all have large bellies and the people serving them have larger ones.

Several minutes later we're back in the car, downing the Italian Frisco Crispy Chicken with added cholesterol, and the "monster-sized" Crispy Curled Frisco Onion Rings with added heart attack. Halfway through my moveable feast, I get a wave of nausea and take a no-fried-food vow. — but what else is there to eat?

DAY 3: Our storm-chasers get an early start at 7 a.m. and drive straight to the only place that's open — where else? — the take-out window at Wendy's. They don't serve breakfast so everyone orders a cup of chili'n'cheese.

I try some in the car but — McDonald's food innovators please note — the combination of beans and bouncing does not make for dashboard dining delight. I give up and hold out for lunch.

3:45 p.m: Ravenous, I pull into Lamar, Nebraska, where we try a fast food Mexican place called Taco John's. I drive out clutching an El Grande Burrito stuffed with sour cream, lettuce and an unidentified meat substance.

A University of Kansas study reveals that one in ten American meals are now eaten while driving, so a lot of people's clothing must be as messy as mine after El Grande Burrito spills on my lap. My pants look like the "before" part of a Tide commercial.

DAY4: We still haven't seen any tornadoes but we've survived eleven consecutive fast-food meals. They're a blur of Taco Bell tacos, Burger King Whoppers, Shari's fajita wraps and something called a Tomahawk-burger, served by a mid-west gas station chain.

The smell of grease permeates our car and clothing, and makes us nauseous even when we aren't eating. I've consumed nine packs of cashews and my healthiest meal was a lettuce enchilada. My stomach should be X-rayed by Health Canada, my cholesterol level placed in a space capsule for future generations to examine.

I'm an experiment in junk food survival and while I'm alive to tell the tale, I'm not sure for how long.

FIVE

Dangerous Canadian Content

THE LOONY LOSES

❖

Prime Minister Jean Chrétien may not be concerned about our Incredible Shrinking Dollar, but the rest of us are, as our currency threatens to become the ruble of the West. We can't have a Russian-style bank run, because there aren't any bank branches left to give us back our money — but it would still be chaos if we all lined up at bank machines and took out $500 every twenty-four hours.

I don't know whether the loony's dive is as good for tourism as our government says, but it's certainly good for U.S. tourists. In recent months, Americans are reported to be buying up all our antique cars and furniture, as well as anything else that isn't nailed down.

"Hi, my name is Bob and I'd like to buy your symphony orchestra."

Economists blame the loony's collapse on everything from NAFTA and the Asian flu to El Niño, but I have my own theory about why the world has lost confidence in our money — they don't trust its name. Our dollar's value has gotten progressively worse since it became known as the "loony."

When the coin was first issued some twelve years ago it was worth close to eighty cents, but it's been in free fall ever since. In the tough new world of global finance, who trusts a "loony"? Look at traditional world currencies such as the mark, the franc and the British pound—all boasting solid, no-nonsense names.

The American "greenback" sounds as dependable as John Wayne, while the Japanese yen creates an appetite for more. Next to the loony the peso sounds dignified while the ruble and the zloty sound like safe places to invest your money.

How can anyone take our currency seriously? Why didn't we just name it the "dummy," or the "wacky," or the "turkey"? Just imagine international currency traders as they buy and sell Canadian dollars on the trading floor:

"Ok, Giles, I got an offer to buy here of 66.28 on the Canadian loo — (giggle, giggle) — on the Canadian — (chortle, chortle) — ohhh god....Giles, I just can't sell that stuff with a straight face."

Admit it, fellow Canadians. In the lean, mean world of global markets this bird can't fly. We need a new name, a new symbol that creates confidence in Canada's currency. If we must have an animal on our coin why make it the loon, a graceful but delicate creature, ill-suited to a time when bulls and bears stalk world currency markets? These days, money talks, it doesn't squawk.

But what animal can we use? The buck and the bald eagle are already taken by our southern neighbors; the beaver is passé, a decent, industrious creature neither bold nor aggressive enough for our entrepreneurial times; the "salmon" or the "trout" sound fishy, though Newfoundland's famous fish would make a nice motto for the back of the coin: "In cod we trust(ed)."

The polar bear decorating the $2 coin has the right heft, but I don't think we should call our currency the "bear." It sounds like it's losing money already. Perhaps the "bull" would be better; I know it's not a Canadian animal, but it does have that ring of success. I can hear the Canada Savings Bond ads: "The bull is on the rampage. Be bullish — buy Canadian."

The "lion" might be fine too if it were indigenous to Canada, so how about settling for the "cougar"? It would sound good on those hourly CNN money reports.

"Good evening. The Canadian cougar leapt in value yesterday and was back on the attack again today, tearing its way through world money markets and devouring other currencies, including the skittish American buck."

Sorry, just dreaming.

Then again, we could also go with a more traditional national symbol. The Canadian "shield" would make a solid-sounding coin, while the "rocky" has a nice ring too, though perhaps a trifle unstable.

We could also move into sports like the Irish did when they nicknamed their pound the "punt." Perhaps we could replace the Queen on our coins with a stronger image, like strongman Louis Cyr ("the Louis"?). Or just take advantage of our national sport.

If we put a hockey stick on the back of our coin everyone in the world would know who it belonged to: that's all they think we do, anyway. Then we could put some hockey legends on the other side to give each denomination its nickname.

The "Rocket" would be a good name for our dime. The "Pocket Rocket" could be our nickel. The "Orr" would be our dollar.

Then again, maybe our dollar should just be called "the puck," a name whose solid Canadian reputation would put an end to our curreny's slide for good. After all, the puck stops here.

OPERATION BEAVER STORM

❖

The U.S. had been trying to bully Canadian business into getting out of Cuba, but President Bill Clinton suddenly started backtracking after Canada threatened to retaliate with our secret weapon: senior citizens. A coalition of Canadian retiree groups warned the U.S. we'd launch a tourist boycott of Florida, a threat that apparently helped turn the tide.

While details were not released I've learned that the Florida threat was part of a large offensive, secretly orchestrated by the Canadian government. The scenario outlined to the Americans was a phase-by-phase operation that made the Yanks think twice. I have possession of secret cabinet documents outlining the full plan, code-named Operation Beaver Storm. Here are the details:

Phase 1. Stop The Snowbirds: Canada would order all its U.S.-bound snowbirds grounded, a devastating blow that would make Hurricane Bertha seem like a summer breeze. Some two million Canadians visit Florida each year, spending two billion Canadian dollars — but that would dry up fast once Operation Beaver Storm started.

Hundreds of hotels from one end of Florida to the other would be deserted once Quebecers failed to show up. A thousand "early-bird-special" restaurants would go belly up. Every windsurf and water-sport company in the state would go under, because no one but Canadians ever steps into the ocean.

There would also be a desperate shortage of crime victims. Florida muggers would be reduced to mugging native Floridians and even each other.

- *OK, gimme your wallet.*
- *No, you gimme yours.*
- *I asked first.*

Alberta and B.C. snowbirds would simultaneously pull out of Arizona and other southwestern states, closing down every bingo parlor, lawn-bowling green and golf course in the region. As Canada took back its old people, the U.S. would go into a major recession: it would be Bye Bye La Floride, adieu Maine, adios Arizona.

Phase 2. Canadian Yankees Come Home: We stopped the Spanish from trawling for turbot, a fish most Canadians had never heard of before. Yet for decades, we've let the U.S. poach bigger fish — our talent.

America steals our doctors, lawyers, newsreaders, movie stars and athletes. Disney has bought a piece of the Cirque de Soleil, and the image of the Mounties. Coca-Cola just bought up Quebec's Naya water. Our drain is their brains.

Operation Beaver Storm would plug the drain for good. We would immediately put up signs at the border saying NO POACHING and seize any U.S. entertainment agent who came across the border scouting for Canadians. Hollywood-bound Canadians would be frisked and forced to leave their talent at the border.

We'd also launch legal action to repatriate famous Canadian stars already in the U.S., such as Morley Safer and Peter Jennings. Hollywood stars Jim Carey, Michael J. Fox and William Shatner would be recalled from Hollywood. America's hottest " babe," Pamela Lee Anderson, would be pulled from "Baywatch" to appear in a parka in a remake of "North of 60." The U.S. music industry would lose k.d. lang, Shania Twain, and Melissa Auf der Maur.

In addition, Canada would take back its most important contribution to the American entertainment industry: hockey. Under Operation Beaver Storm, we would repatriate all Canadian hockey players living in the U.S., from Patrick Roy to the man they call Mario " Lemioo."

Meanwhile Brian Tobin would take a fleet of Coast Guard infantry down to Colorado to seize the Stanley Cup they won several years ago. After all, the Nordiques are our team anyway. Sure, they're called the Colorado Avalanche and they like it down there, but we'd bring them back to Canadian soil and ask questions later.

Phase 3. Retaking Canadian Bacon: America's Cuba policy is based on old history: the fact the U.S. owned most of Cuba before Castro's revolution. But if the U.S. is going to invoke ownership rights going back thirty-six years ago, why not go even further back? That's exactly what Operation Beaver Storm proposes.

Under Phase 3, Canada would join England in suing the U.S. for the thirteen colonies England lost during the American Revolution. Canada would also demand back any goods or intellectual property the U.S. has stolen from us in the last 129 years. For instance, we invented basketball and Superman. We'd demand them back, plus royalties.

We'd also take back the rights to other important Canadian inventions. Snowmobiles. Frozen fish. Mashed potatoes. Canadian bacon. The Zamboni machine. Not to mention Daylight-Saving time — also invented by Canadians. As a result, the U.S. would be forced to live on standard time all year round — and get out of bed in the dark all winter.

Given the above scenario, it's easy to see why Clinton took the smart way out and backed down. The U.S. came perilously close to losing some of the best things about the American way of life.

Us.

HOME GROAN

❖

Summer is ending, the leaves are changing colours and one of the best gardening seasons in years is over. Thank goodness. I won't have to hear any more stories about my friends' fennel gardens, or their electronic seed catalogues, or their battle against field mice, potato bugs, and whatever other herbivores they've been fighting to a standoff.

This has been a summer of lawn order and I, for one, can use a break. Everywhere I go people are hunched over the soil, seeding, planting and harvesting. Every time I turn on the TV there's some bright-eyed "Canadian Gardener" encouraging me to grow my own eggplant. Here in Montreal, people are so obsessed with greenery they've elected a gardener as mayor.

Gardening may be one of the fastest-growing trends around but it's not growing on me. Frankly, when I look at a lawn I see a place to put a lawn chair. When I pass a community garden, I see a botanical penal colony. Sorry to be prickly, but refusing to garden is in my roots.

I come from a long line of urbanites who moved from town to town across eastern Europe trying to avoid rural labour. My great-great-grandfather fled the Russian countryside for the city so his descendants wouldn't have to stoop in the fields and get their hands dirty. They'd be able to buy their vegetables wholesale.

Later generations lived up to his dream. My grandmother had a black thumb and could kill vegetables just by making a salad. My mom was a gourmet cook, but our back yard was always a vegetable-free zone. There are no farmers in the Freed family. We like our flowers in a vase and our lettuce from a bin, preferably wrapped in its natural covering: cellophane.

I can understand people who grew up in the countryside and have a long-standing relationship with the land, but in recent years gardening is becoming a mass trend. An entire generation of baby-boomers is going back to roots they never had. Many successful professionals I know now grow their own soup and salad on the back porch.

When I ask my friends what's gotten into them they get misty-eyed and even mystical. They talk about the miracle of the seasons and the zen of zucchini. They talk about the process of creating what they eat and look at me like I'm an insensitive oaf who takes his vegetables for granted.

I guess I do. I don't need to understand agriculture to eat a salad anymore than I need to understand electricity to turn on the hall lights. I flip the switch and the room gets bright. I'm sure it would be satisfying to dam a river, build my own electrical pylons and produce my own power, but I prefer to leave it to Hydro-Québec.

Urban life is difficult enough without looking for additional challenges; finding a parking spot outside the supermarket is challenging enough. I'm a city boy, even when I go to the country. I'm willing to rough it, but only as far as my extension cord will reach.

Despite gardening's growth, I worry the trend is just beginning. Like anything that involves baby-boomers gardening will probably boom too, sprouting a hundred lucrative off-shoots. There will be books on "How to Grow the Perfect Arugula" and car tapes for the "executive gardener" who wants to increase his "herb power."

There will be fitness courses in aerobic gardening, with special ten-pound pruning shears that allow you to " tone and till" at the same time. They will include lower-body weeding courses with catchy names like "Heave and Hoe" and "Rake and Roll." Someone will invent a combination lawn mower and StairMaster to help you keep as trim as your garden: The LawnMaster.

Maybe I'm being a little cynical, or maybe I'm just in gardening denial, and some day I too will suddenly see the value of stooping in the soil. I'll be sitting in a restaurant eating a chicken-salad sandwich when the truth hits me. I'll realize it's time to start being interested in the process, not just the product.

And I'll start growing my own chicken salad.

OUTWITTING WINTER

❖

I WAS CHATTING OUTSIDE with a next-door neighbor this week, but to look at us you'd have thought we lived on different continents. She was dressed like Nanook of the North, without an inch of exposed flesh visible between her Arctic parka hood and her knee-high winter boots. I was dressed in a light cotton sweater, with sneakers and no gloves.

It reminded me that winter is a state of mind as much as a time of year, and we all have our own ways of surviving it. There are many psychological models for getting through the Canadian winter, among them:

The Cautious Canuck: This person lays down the winter matting on their stairs in late July. They've done all their winter shopping by August to beat the crowds, and have their snow tires installed on Labour Day.

By the time their kids start school, their boots and mittens are out in the hall, arranged in order by the thickness of their fibre: Gore-Tex, Velcro, Hollofil, Thinsulate, polypropylene. This year's winter vacation was booked before last year's was over, which is why the rest of us can never get a last-minute flight.

This type resents when winter starts late abecause their winter windshield wipers don't work well in the rain. "I can't believe this," one such friend complained. "I bought this great pair of winter boots at full price in September, and by the time I get to wear them, they'll be on Christmas sale!"

The Canadian Gladiator: This type is out to conquer winter and is prepared for every eventuality, from a freak July snowstorm to a power blackout stretching from New York to James Bay. His 4x4 Cherokee Jeep Avalanche Snowslayer is equipped with twin-block heaters, six-inch-spike wheels and enough salt to melt a route to the North Pole.

His trunk is an arsenal of scrapers, shovels and other Canadian Tire products arranged in alphabetical order, while his supply of flares could light up an airport runway during a blackout. On snowy days, he also carries traction bars, a tow cable and an industrial battery jumper he's dying for a chance to use. He loves to sidle up to neighbors when they're stalled in a November snowstorm and say: "Hi. Need a boost?"

When the first storm hits, The Gladiator and the Cautious Canuck are flying high, because they're months ahead of the crowd, but they'll have to pay for their enthusiasm later. By January they will be sick of worrying about winter and by February they will be totally depressed. "God, this winter feels like it's lasted all year," they will say, and for them, it has.

During the first thaw, they will start preparing their summer gear, and by early March, they will have their air conditioner installed in the window.

The Procrastinator: The most common winter types, these step-by-steppers adapt to the climate only when there is no choice. When their fingers turn white, they go shopping for gloves; when their car is snowed in, they get the shovel out of the shed — after shovelling their way in with a broom.

When the snow on their steps melts in a January thaw, they finally get around to laying down their winter carpet. They give up summer reluctantly, bit by bit. "Look, honey, the steaks have started to re-freeze since I put them on the grill. I guess there aren't too many weeks of barbecuing left."

They rarely remember to buy a scraper for the car until they've spent the night hacking ice off their windshield with a credit card. And when they put the new scraper away in the back shed at the end of winter, they find the one from last year, beside the one from the year before.

Their behavior is driven by denial, an unwillingness to confront winter until they absolutely have to. They secretly hope that if they ignore winter long enough, it will be over.

The Hibernator: These rare but fascinating types refuse to admit that winter exists at all, because they never go outside to find out. Hibernators usually live downtown and spend winter going from office to car to bar to bed; the only reason they step outside is to take a taxi to the subway.

You can spot them easily because they wear summer shoes and windbreakers in February. They don't own gloves, unless friends have bought them as a birthday present. If they take a vacation in winter, it's only to get away — not escape the cold; they're just as likely to vacation in Oslo, as in Florida, because they won't be going outside there either.

So choose a winter strategy that works for your type of personality and stick with it until the snow melts. Remember that everyone faces death in their own way — and the same is true of winter.

But at least winter has a happier ending.

SNOWBUSTERS

❖

THE BLIZZARD OF '96 is over and amazingly, Washington and New York are still standing. As I watched American TV coverage this week, I didn't think either city would survive.

The blizzard got live catastrophe coverage on CNN and took up more space in American newspapers than earthquakes and entire wars on other continents. Many newscasters called it the "Blizzard of the Century" and given American hyperbole, we're lucky they stopped there. It could easily have become the Blizzard of the Millennium, or the Biggest Whiteout Since the Ice Age.

Reporters weren't the only ones in a panic. Many cities closed airports and schools and banned cars from the streets. The legendary U.S. mail closed down, and will now have to rewrite its motto:

Neither rain nor sleet nor hail
will stop the U.S. mail.
but occasionally in blizzards,
we fail.

The real trouble wasn't the Blizzard of '96; it was American weather wimps who freak out over weather that's routine in Canada. Sure twenty inches is a lot of snow, but at least there wasn't a blue-collar strike like Montrealers get routinely during storms.

A friend was in New York during the storm and says the only problem was New Yorkers. They don't own basic winter battle gear like scrapers, winter tires, or even shovels. Some of them were digging out their cars with tennis racquets.

To boot, nobody knows how to drive in winter. They floor the gas when they're stuck on ice and they don't even know how to rock a car out of a snow drift — a Canadian skill so basic our PM recently used it as a metaphor for constititutional change.

"You know, the constitution is like getting your car out of a snowbank in winter," said Mr. Chrétien. "You go a little bit forward, then a little bit backward, then forward, then backward, then forward, then backward

— and pretty soon you're out!"

Americans obviously needed the help of Canadian experts and that's a shame, because many of us were ready for duty. Fighting winter is one thing we Canucks do better than anyone in the world, so why don't we put our experience to work? We send peacekeeping troops to Bosnia carrying guns, which few Canadians know anything about, yet we were born with snow shovels in our hands.

It's time to create a Canadian Snowkeeping Force, an emergency force that fights dangerous blizzards all over the world. I can already see a fleet of Hercules aircraft landing at Washington's Dulles airport during a big storm and unloading a thousand trucks, snowblowers and sidewalk-clearers. Crowds of thankful Americans would be waiting at the runway to applaud them, waving maple leafs flags and singing "The Canucks are Coming."

Our boys would hand out trinkets like lock de-icer and jumper cables, then move into action, boosting batteries, digging out cars and barking commands. "Forward, Forward! STOP! Now straighten your wheels...baaack up...easy on the gas — NO! Don't spin your tires!"

Once our reputation as blizzard-busters was established, we could create spin-off industries, like Americans who have cashed in on the Green Berets and Desert Storm. U.S. military magazines advertise machine guns "as used by the U.S. army in Asia and the Gulf War."

We could advertise RXB-27 Snowblowers and CF-19 Snowslayer Shovels "as used by Canadian Snowkeepers in the Blizzard of the Century." Or Gander goosedown parkas, "guaranteed to protect you through Canadian winters 199 out of 200 times! Tested by live Canadians!"

Just as Hollywood has glorified the U.S. military for decades, we could turn out Canadian films based on our military storm exploits. How about *Snow Hard 2* or *Top Shovel*? Or *The Legend of the White Berets: Snowkeepers of the Planet*?

UNINVENTIVE THINKING

❖

I RECENTLY READ ABOUT a new suitcase invented in Tokyo that converts into a miniature car that travels 6.5 miles an hour.

It's called the "dream luggage." Apparently, the wheels pop down along with a gearstick and steering wheel — and it's ready to roll. I'd buy one tomorrow, but they still have a few kinks to work out. For instance, the suitcase weighs 32 kg, twice the usual airline allowance for luggage.

As well, it costs several million yen, about the same price as a luxury car.

Despite these problems, I'm incredibly impressed by people who try to invent things like "driveable luggage." If you left it to me, it wouldn't make its appearance for another ten or twenty thousand years. When it comes to inventing, there are two kinds of people — and I'm the non-inventing kind.

I sit in the kitchen peeling and mashing potatoes and think: "Geez, there's *got* to be an easier way to do this." Then I keep peeling.

But another type of person is doing exactly the same thing and thinks: "I can build a way better potato!" And thus was born instant mashed potatoes, in 1961, one of a long line of great Canadian inventions.

The key to successful inventing is figuring out what *you* need, then assuming that everyone else can use one too. It's a risky business.

For every Walter Edison who's famous, there's a Ralph Edison who isn't.

You have to be bold. As I sit here grumbling, people who are confident about the shape of the future are out there busily inventing the necessities of tomorrow: the electric snow shovel. The glow-in-the-dark toilet. The voice-activated microwave.

"OK, do the peas and broccoli — and this time, don't make them soggy!"

I have no end of things I need, but I'm usually too caught up in my problems to think about solutions. Ever since I bought my first VCR ten years ago, I've spent half my TV time looking under the sofa for the remote control. It never occurred to me to invent a way to find it. I always figured I was the only idiot who lost it.

Then recently, I read about a survey by Magnavox that showed more than half the population loses their remotes regularly — some as often as ten times a week. Three out of ten people surveyed said they generally found it under the living room couch. One in five said they frequently found it in the kitchen or bathroom; another 6% found it in the refrigerator, 4% in the garbage, 3% outdoors and 2% in their cars.

It turned out I wasn't as dumb as I thought — I was just a typical TV watcher, although I seem to be the only one who finds his remote in the rice cooker.

Magnavox has just put an alarm in its TV remotes that makes a beeping noise when you push a button on your TV. So get ready to hear a lot of beeping fridges.

Despite my uninventiveness, Canada is a nation of inventors. Over 30,000 Canadians a year apply for patents, one of the highest per capita rates in the world. We invented the snowmobile, insulin, and the railway sleeping car. We invented gingerale, frozen fish, the paint roller, and the green garbage bag. We've invented all kinds of idiotic activities to while away the winter, from table hockey and five-pin bowling to first ministers' conferences.

Some say our inventiveness is due to our long winters, when there's nothing else to do but sit around and build a better moosetrap. Or dream about a remote-controlled lawnmower. So if any of you aspiring Canadian inventors out there are wondering what to invent this winter, here are some necessities we non-inventing types could use:

I can live without a cordless toaster or a laser razor, but I'd love a device that automatically removes rotting leftovers from my fridge. How about a parking spot detector that notifies you as soon as there's a free spot in the area you're driving.

"Parking space now empty on Ste. Catherine St. west of Peel. Back up now...Now!...Faster!!

"Sorry, slowpoke — it's gone."

Finally, if they can invent a TV remote-finder why not apply the same science to finding other stuff messy people like me are always losing. Many Canadians lose hours each month looking for their keys, eyeglasses, scarfs, socks, and umbrellas.

When you leave a restaurant without your umbrella, *it* should find you: "Josh, you're leaving the twenty-foot range. It's raining — you need me!"

I've got lots of other ideas for inventive souls out there eager to design things people need. Just don't ask for my help in inventing them. I've always subscribed to Murphy's Law of Design: Anytime I can understand how something works, it's already obsolete.

CHICKENS 'R' US

❖

THE RCMP ARE BACK IN BUSINESS as a brave symbol of Canada's national defense, but they've certainly changed their image. Meet the Royal Canadian Mounted Poultry, a crack regiment of chickens that's been stationed at the Canadian border to fend off an invasion from the U.S.

These brave Canadian birds aren't protecting us against bombers or missiles, but from another airborne threat: American killer mosquitoes carrying West Nile disease, which has killed seven people in New York City. Now there's fear the mosquitoes may be headed north to slip across our notoriously porous border and prey on Canadians in cottage country.

But there's no need for panic. Our federal government's has stationed 34 brigades of birds along the border to detect the killer mosquitoes the moment they penetrate our line: DEW line of kamikaze chickens spread out from New Brunswick to B.C., ready to lay down their lives for their country.

So far, not much is known about these plucky Canadian conscripts. Are they issued OFF!? Have they been trained in the martial arts? Do they wear uniforms? — or is white skin and a red comb enough to show they serve Canada?

There's something about these brave birds I find fittingly Canadian, and their courage should give us pause. If they are bitten and die in the line of service, how will we honor them? Will we bury them or barbecue them? Should we make them the guests of honor at an official state dinner?

It's time we showed some new respect for these cocky Canadians. As it stands, we pay them chicken feed, fricassee their relatives and tell silly jokes about chickens crossing the road. Worst of all, we stereotype their entire species as...chicken. But these bold conscripts may soon change our image of them from cowards to heroes, creating new expressions like: "as courageous as a chicken," and "as heroic as a hen."

In fact, our new flock of border guards is only the latest sign of the fast-rising status of the chicken, a proud new symbol of the 2000s. Look around and you'll see chickens everywhere.

One of the hottest films at the box office is Chicken Run, about some hens who make a great escape from a poultry farm, under the leadership of a rooster known as the "Lone Free-Ranger."

Meanwhile, in British Columbia, there was a recent front-page story about a chicken that made a real run for freedom. It bolted from a poultry farm and was adopted by picketing workers outside, who made it their union mascot.

According to the strikers, "Bruce the Chicken" is a metaphor for the plight of mistreated poultry workers everywhere, who are presumably fattened up, then slaughtered. Chickens 'R' Us, say the workers.

Chicken is also increasingly popular at the Canadian dinner table as people shun beef, frightened by e-coli, Mad Cow disease and runaway cholesterol. Many families now eat Friday night chicken seven nights a week for health reasons, treating the bird as if it was the broccoli of the meat world.

Whether grain-fed, Kentucky Fried or just roasted, chicken is in, and it's time to recognize its status as an important national symbol. The maple leaf is wilting, the beaver is a pest and the moose is a rarity few urbanites will encounter, unless they hit one on the highway. Yet the chicken is a common and ever more popular Canadian animal that's found in every corner of the country, including Quebec, where it has its own distinct flavour — St. Hubert barbecued.

It's time we honored the brave Canadian fighting chicken. Let's put one on the back of a coin, or even on our hundred-dollar bill. Let's make it our national bird, our national animal, our national dish.

The Russians have their bear, the British their bulldog and the Americans their eagle. Now we Canadians have our chicken, a strutting symbol that may soon deserve a place in our national anthem. Perhaps we could use it to replace one of those endlessly repetitive "We stand on guard for thees" at the end of "O Canada."

In fact, let's try it out now. Everyone, sing after me:

O Canada
Glorious and free!
O Canada, we stand on guard for thee,
Ohhhh Canada, we are the RCM-Poultry!

SIX

Neverendum Againdum

SOPHIST'S CHOICE

❖

Beep.

Welcome to Interactive Neverendum Referendum, the exciting multiple-choice question that allows you to choose your own country, province, state, republic, kingdom, duchy, nation...
Please stay on the line to make your selection — as long as it isn't NO.

Beep. What language do you wish to communicate in:
1 - French
2 - French

Beep. Thank you for choosing French.
Please select one of the following options:

Do you want Quebec to be:
1 - Sovereign, proud and free
0 - Just another province like Prince Edward Island

Beep. You have pressed 0.
Perhaps you did not understand the question. Let us re-phrase it:

Do you want Quebec to be:
1 - Sovereign and free, with Canadian passport and Canadian dollar but no Canadian debt
0 - The same old humiliating status quo we've had since the Plains of Abraham

Beep. Sorry, you have pressed 0 again.
This choice is humiliating and invalid. Are you sure of your selection? To help you make a more educated choice, we will provide a special Neverendum Referendum tutorial.

Beep.
For a tutorial on sovereignty, please select 1.
For a tutorial on federalism, please move to Alberta.

Beep. Thank you for choosing 1.
Welcome to the Sovereignty Tutorial, which will help you understand the complex issues behind the coming Quebec referendum. Please listen carefully:

The Québecois people are a nation. They have been humiliated by the English from the Durham report to the 1982 Night of the Long Knives to the savage attack on the fleur-de-lis in Brockville, Ontario. The Parti Québecois is finally giving Quebecers the opportunity to become normal. This is a historic moment.
We now return to the main menu.

Please select:

1 - A Sovereign, Free and Normal Quebec Nation
0 - A colonized, stagnant, truncated Quebec in Canada

Beep. You have chosen 0 *again.*

Who are you? Where were you born?
Perhaps it would be best if you didn't vote at all. Maybe you should consider abstaining so that old-stock members of the majority who understand Quebec's humiliation can make a more informed choice. This would be very patriotic and prove you have what it takes to become a good citizen of Quebec, after it is a nation.

Beep! Beep! Beep! Beep!
SYSTEM MALFUNCTION! SYSTEM MALFUNCTION!

The offensive statement above appeared due to a glitch in our computer system. The Parti Québecois, the Bloc Québecois and all other Québecois wish to disassociate themselves from these comments. Every Quebec citizen is a Québecois — even if they don't vote like one.

Beep. Please answer the following multiple-choice question. This time you *must* say YES.

1 - YES! I want a sovereign Quebec with Canadian dollar and subsidized Quebec Winter Olympics

2 - YES! I want a sovereign Quebec with no debt and no winter

3 - YES! I want negotiations for a better deal *inside* Canada. (If these negotiations are not complete within two weeks, Quebec will reluctantly declare itself sovereign and free.)

Beep. You have not made a selection. Please choose one of the above.

Beep. Please reply or we will continue to ask this question again and again and again until you say YES!
Please choose now.

Beep. You have attempted to hang up. Sorry, this option is not available. You must say YES! to one of the above options.

Say YES.
Say YES now.
YES!YES!YES!YES!YES!YES!YES!YES!

Please say Yes. Pretty please. Pretty, pretty please.

Beep. Sorry, you have failed to make a selection — for now.
You must return to the main menu.

Beep. Welcome to Interactive Neverendum Referendum, the exciting mutiple-choice question that that allows you to choose your own country, province, state, republic, kingdom, duchy, nation...
Please stay on the line to make your selection...

REFERENDUM RUNUP

❖

[JULY 1995] THE REFERENDUM CAMPAIGN hasn't officially started yet but the first tanks are rumbling down Canadian streets. Fortunately, they are Canadian tanks — think tanks — that cause more distraction than destruction.

The opening salvo was fired last week by the C.D. Howe Institute, a powerful Canadian think tank that can launch a study heard right across the country. It's popular with federalist forces but doesn't frighten Quebec separatists who don't trust its long-range accuracy.

Howe fired off the standard verbal ammunition meant to rattle civilians: Quebec independence would lead to economic and legal chaos, rising interest rates and a massive decline in the Canadian loony, beaver and moose.

Yawn. It was meant to be a bombshell but in Montreal it had the impact of a BB gun. French newspapers like *La Presse* carried the story on the inside pages and it didn't even rank as anglophone dinner conversation.

Everyone was talking about the really important news — the end of the strike by our hockey players.

Quebecers of every persuasion are a battle-hardened lot accustomed to the sound of exploding studies and heavy think-tank fire. As veterans of the Meech Morass, the Charlottetown Disaccord and dozens of others constitutional firestorms, we go by the old adage: "Figures can lie and liars can figure" — and if you don't like these figures, you can always find some others.

Separatist forces responded to the C.D. Howe study with a fierce anti-think-tank barrage. Jacques Brassard, the PQ's Minister of Verbal Overkill, accused the Howe study of "economic and political terrorism."

Terrorism? This must be the only place in the world lucky enough to be terrorized by economists.

The skirmish is only the start of what will be another very Canadian war, fought with words not weapons, committees not combat troops. We will fire off memos. We will drop constitutional bombshells. We will pummel each other with polls, and strafe each other with statistics.

It could be worse. If Russian leader Boris Yeltsin were Canadian he'd probably have sat on a think tank instead of standing up on a real one when he seized Moscow. I still remember Maj.-Gen. Lewis Mac-Kenzie, Canadian commander of UN forces in former Yugoslavia, when he said:

"If Bosnians were Canadians, we'd simply take the whole population and bore them to death with conferences."

So prepare to be bored. It's going to get noisier and noisier. Soon both sides will be rolling out more think-tanks and related weaponry: StatsCan studies, Revenue Quebec reports, bank bulletins, investment reviews, committee papers and other fearful facts.

A federalist study will show that separatism would cause so many Quebecers to flee to western Canada that the entire country will tilt sideways, causing major flooding in Vancouver. Meanwhile a study of Canadian anthems will show that only 15% of Quebecers feel "O Canada" pulls on their heart strings, while another 15% choose "Gens du Pays."

The remaining 70% will choose the sound of the bugle at NHL hockey games.

After the studies will come the next wave of verbal artillery — an aerial barrage that pummels us with polls and pounds us with punditry. There will be no end of work for pollsters, TV analysts, experts, critics, political scientists, sociologists, economists, and astrologists like Jojo. There will be partisan TV ads with testimonials by doctors, lawyers, farmers, plumbers and rock stars, saying things like "Music sounds better in a separate Quebec."

There will be violent televised debates over who keeps what if Quebec secedes. Who gets the airports and seaways? Who gets the debt? Who gets the Montreal Canadiens? Who gets Schwartz's deli?

As the decibel level rises, we will fool the world into believing this is a trouble spot, again. European journalists will fly into Quebec in their flak jackets eager to know the reported death count.

"You mean the debt count," we will tell them. "It's up to $40 billion and rising!"

Foreign reporters will rush about the streets looking for bombs, bullets and other traditional signs of battle. To no avail. There will be only one brief outburst of Canadian-style terrorism when three teenagers in Speckled Trout, Manitoba are found stomping on a Quebec flag. The fuss will die down when reporters discover all three are members of the PQ, on a "fact-finding" mission for Premier Jacques Parizeau.

After all the sound and fury, Quebecers will go to the polls on referendum day and vote exactly as expected. Separatists will vote yes, federalists will vote no and the final count will be 60-40 in favor of Canada, without a single vote swayed by all the noise.

The battle will be over for awhile, but the think-tanks won't stop firing.

ROOTS, SHMOOTS

❖

Dear Jacques Parizeau,

As Ed Sullivan might have said 25 years ago, that was "a really big show" you put on last Wednesday to introduce your party's new Declaration of Independence, setting the stage for the coming referendum campaign.

Gilles Vigneault waxed poetic about the beauties of winter. Young Quebec actors read emotionally about fishing and ploughing the soil. There were pictures of farms and sunsets and lots of talk about solitude and harvesting. It was very romantic — but not very representative of many of us who have spent our lives here in Montreal.

The Declaration of Independence seemed to be written by someone who had never left Quebec City and never set foot on Ste. Catherine Street. It talked a lot about winter but never mentioned ball hockey. It talked about our farms, but never mentioned our festivals.

It seemed aimed at Quebecers who live in the countryside and spend their lives in the fields. But what about the three million of us who live in and around Montreal? Where were we? It certainly wasn't my heritage you were describing in the preamble. For example:

The time has come to reap the fields of history... To harvest what has been sown for us by four hundred years of men and women and courage, rooted in the soil.

To be honest, my family has been in Quebec for 100 years, but we haven't done much harvesting, unless you count raspberry-picking on weekends in the Laurentians. My ancestors were not *rooted in the soil;* they rooted on the back balcony where they spent most of their time yakking with the neighbors.

My grandfather had a "Victory Garden" during W.W. II, but it was a grim thing, as lifeless as a graveyard. A cat kept eating the sprouts, until our dog killed it right on top of the tomato patch and my grandfather got depressed and gave up gardening for good.

My family never fished or trapped either, unless you count my uncle, who took the streetcar out to Maisonneuve market every Saturday to hunt for fresh chicken on the back of farmers' trucks.

As you may have guessed, I come from a long line of urbanites: hardened Montrealers who would need a lot of changes in your new declaration before they felt comfortable with it. For example: *We know the winter in our souls. We know its blustery days, its solitude, its false eternity and its apparent deaths.*

Well, maybe that's true in Lac St. Jean but not over here where I live near St. Laurent Blvd. We're more familiar with winter traffic jams, and the sound of the snowblowers as they seal our cars behind a wall of snow only minutes after we've dug them out.

Yes, *we know what it is to be bitten by the winter cold,* but why not add: *and that is why we wear cheap rabbit fur hats, long underwear, and Gore-tex mitts and keep jumper cables in the trunk.*

I know that "winter is my country" but unlike Mr. Vigneault, sometimes, during February cold spells, I wish it wasn't.

Because the heart of this land beats in French and because that heartbeat is as meaningful as the seasons that hold sway over it.

I agree again but I think that *many other languages are the veins and arteries of this land…and even the tiny apostrophe has its place.*

While I'm at it, here are a few other phrases I would add to the new Declaration of Independence to make it feel more like my homeland.

"We, the men and women of Montreal love this place and all its festivities: from the Fête de la St. Jean to the Fête du Homard; from St. Patrick's Day to July 1st Moving Day, when we carry a fridge instead of a flag; from 6 a.m. sunrise at the look-out to the 3 a.m traffic jam on Ste. Catherine Street.

"We love the solitude of mornings on Mount Royal but also the squeal of the taxi, the squawk of the pigeon and the thunder of 1000 jackhammers during pothole season. We even love the wail of the city's towtrucks as they haul our cars away after a snowstorm.

"We, the courageous men and women of Montreal have survived unimaginable perils: from the traffic on the Decarie Circle and Turcotte interchange to the mysteries of the Louis-Hippolyte Lafontaine tunnel, where we still grope to understand the signs saying ETEIGNEZ VOS PHARES.

"We have celebrated the ethnic heritage that is Montreal. We have eaten the felafel of Faillon Street, the manicotti of Mozart Street, and the smoked meat of the Main. We have savoured the croissant of Rue St. Denis and the *frites* of Ontario East — but on Sundays we do Chinese.

"We the men and women of this place love our city and our province, especially in early spring when clothing comes off and café-terrace chairs come out. We love Montreal...

> *We love her on the Main and in the rain*
> *In the snow and the Metro*
> *From downtown to the burbs, and then some*
> *Yes, even during the referendum.*"

OTTAWA NOs BEST

❖

PREMIER JACQUES PARIZEAU has been brandishing a secret federal document all week that certainly looks important. That's because the word SECRET is stamped in big letters on every page, like something out of "Get Smart."

In fact, most of the document's information is as exciting as the plans for the 15th annual Beaconsfield Walkathon, but one section is certainly intriguing. The leaked document mentions secret federal plans to promote the "No" side in the referendum, by hiding subliminal messages in all kinds of places.

Among the subliminal campaigns being considered by Ottawa are anti-alcohol and anti-tobacco ads saying things like: NON MERCI and JUST SAY NO. Similarly, Tourism Canada's TV ads for Quebec will be extended past their usual summer run. They won't just be trying to attract tourists to Quebec, but to sell Canada to Quebecers subliminally.

Get real. It's bad enough to have separatist politicians screaming propaganda at us all summer; now we have to worry about subliminal federalist propaganda, too. The federal document refers to "other" subliminal campaigns as well, including the "Bronfman Heritage Foundation ads, the United Nations' 50th anniversary ads, etc."

That "etc." worries me. Where else are they secretly sending me messages? To find out, I called a mole I know in the federal government. He slipped me some recent minutes from the secret Cabinet committee responsible for the subliminal defence of Canada. Here's a copy:

COMMITTEE TO SUBLIMINALLY SAVE CANADA

[TOP TOP TOP SECRET]

CHAIR: Good afternoon, ladies and gentlemen. Thank you for coming to our anonymous little gathering — get it, aNONymous, heh, heh. That's French. Just a little subliminal joke to get things warmed up. No? (Titters.)

CHAIR: As you know, our campaign to save Canada continues on many subliminal fronts and we're here for an update. Let's start with the Save-Canada representative from Tourism Canada.

TOURISM: Well, Madame Chair, as you know from the newspapers, I've already extended Tourism Canada TV for P.E.I. beaches into the fall. Frankly, I'll keep them going until Referendum Day, even if the actors have to wear tuques and nose-warmers.

I also want to announce a new subliminal travel slogan! It will be printed on blue and white billboards and say: "To KNOW Quebec is to LOVE Quebec." In French, it will be: "Quebec! NONchalant."

CHAIR: Hmm, NOT bad. Now, let's hear from our new chief of "slogans for crown corporations."

CROWN CORP: Thank you. We also have something new in the works.

VOICES FROM FLOOR: Shame! Shame! Boo!

CROWN CORP: Pardon me, what did I say?

CHAIR: Sorry, you're new on the subliminal committee — but you'll have to watch your tongue. You used the "oui" word.

CROWN CORP: What word? All I said was: "We also have something... Ohmigod! I'm sorry, I said "we" — or, er, OUI. Don't worry, Madame Chair, it will NOT happen to US again.

CHAIR: Good. Remember: loose lips are subliminal slips! Please continue.

CROWN CORP: As I was saying, I also have something in the works. I'm proud to announce the official new post office slogan:
    "COAST TO COAST with CANADA POST."
We're still working on a French version.

FLOOR: Bravo! Bravo! Formidable!

CHAIR: Excellent work! Now, before we adjourn, let's hear from the Secret Subsidies bureau.

SUBSIDIES: OK, chief. As usual, I'm offering secret subsidies to any company that gives us subliminal help. I've given Canadian Tire the usual bundle for its fall advertising campaign — and I'm ironing out details with Canada Dry and Maple Leaf Bacon this week.

FLOOR: Bravo!

SUBSIDIES: We will also be proposing a new slogan for our national airline:
"AIR CANADA — DON'T LEAVE CANADA WITHOUT IT!"

CHAIR: Good! What about United Airlines?

SUBSIDIES: Well, they're American, but we're in touch with them anyway. We've also made contact with United Way, Canada Packers, and Confederation Life Insurance. However, we still haven't decided between Federal Express and United Parcel Services.

CROWN CORP: Sorry to interrupt — I know I'm new here — but has anyone thought of backing a big campaign for Canada Trust?

FLOOR: (chanting) NO! NO! NO!

CROWN CORP: I'm sorry, did I say something else wrong?

CHAIRMAN: No, not at all. When we really like an idea here, we shout NO! After all, that's our message — isn't it?

CROWN CORP: Yes — Oh, I'm sorry — I mean NO!

FLOOR: NO! NO! NO! NO!

CROWN CORP: NO! NO! NO!

CHAIR: NO! NO! NO! And now, let's sing our team song!

EVERYONE: Uni-i-i-ited we stand!
          Divi-i-i-ided OUI falls...

(Remaining minutes drowned out.)

NEVERENDUM SURVIVAL GUIDE

❖

I WAS HAVING DINNER at a friend's house the other night, and we were happily carrying on a conversation, without once mentioning *the subject*. Suddenly there was the furious sound of hammering outside, so we all went out onto the balcony to see what was happening.

In an empty lot across the street, several men were swinging mallets and erecting a giant billboard. It said "OUIBEC" — a slogan of the Yes side — and our conversation quickly turned to *the subject*. As the referendum noose draws tighter, it's getting harder and harder to escape thinking about it.

Oui and Non signs are taking over every lamppost, metro car, bus, billboard and tree. Mailboxes are stuffed with the new sovereignty bill with an INCREDIBLE NEW PREAMBLE and a special YOU-CAN'T-HAVE-YOUR-CANADIAN-MONEY-BACK offer to Canada.

Newspapers have no other news anymore. From the front page to the business page to the sports page, the referendum is swallowing everything in its vicinity. It has become Quebec's version of the O.J. trial.

The worst part is that the official campaign hasn't even started yet. As the referendum closes in, what can you do to protect yourself? How can you avoid getting numb from the neverendumb? Allow me to offer some survival tips.

1. Leave town: Incredibly, many countries are NOT talking about the referendum. There's still time to take a holiday before referendum charter flights fill. Thousands of snowbirds go south to escape winter. Become a ballot bird.

WARNING: Do not go elsewhere in Canada. Other provinces are even more upset about the referendum than we are. Ontario and the West are depressed about the fragile dollar and the rising rhetoric of Lucien Bouchard. The Maritimes are depressed about everything.

Go elsewhere. The U.S. is still safe to travel in, but that might change as O.J. winds down and Americans look northward for entertainment.

You could find yourself sitting on a Florida beach surrounded by *USA Today* headlines saying: "CANUCK BUCK CHUCKED."

Your best bet to avoid referendum news is to visit a nation that has real problems. Go to Bosnia, Algeria, or other war-torn countries and I guarantee you won't hear a word about our national problems.

2. Pretend to leave town: In the era of global communications, it's possible to stay home and live elsewhere. Simply don't buy the *Gazette*, the *Globe and Mail, La Presse,* or any other Canadian paper. Instead, drop out and plug in. Surf the Internet. Get a shortwave radio and program it to Radio Moscow or Radio Havana. Channel-hop in a 100-channel TV universe with no referendum news at all — from the Surgery Network to the Fishing-With-Dynamite channel.

For added protection, install a children's program lock on your TV and keep out offensive Canadian channels like Newsworld and TVOntario. That way, if you accidentally flick to the CBC, a warning will flash:

"Viewer Discretion Advised.
May Carry Disturbing Referendum Material."

Avoid other places where local reality might intrude, too — like looking at your mail, answering the phone or driving anywhere. If you must go out, look down at the sidewalk at all times to avoid messages on billboards, buses and balconies. In fact, it's probably best to stay indoors until October 30th.

3. Take advantage of the referendum: Believe it or not, many people actually like the sovereignty debate, because they make a killing on it. The referendum industry employs tens of thousands of MPs, MNAs, pollsters, professors, economists, journalists, translators, speechwriters, enumerators, sign-makers, printers, paper-producers and more.

Line up at the trough too. Most of the good jobs are taken, but it's not too late to find yourself a niche. For example: journalists and pollsters are prowling the streets desperately looking for "undecided" voters to interview. Become one!

Call a news conference and announce you are a former federalist who is now undecided. Soon you will be called by CBC producers asking you to participate in interviews, studies and town hall meetings with Peter Mansbridge.

You will become a star, with many long-range possibilities. If there is a narrow victory for either side, and the turmoil continues, you will have a full-time career as a a Professional Undecided Voter.

4. Use psychology: Some people can't stop thinking about the referendum because it slips into their dreams at night. If you are one of them, here is a psychological method to help you get the referendum out of your system.

For one hour every day, force yourself to think about nothing *but* the referendum. Watch Lucien Bouchard on the parliamentary channel while reading *Le Devoir* editorials. Read the PQ's sovereignty bill and memorize the preamble. Think about how the referendum is destroying your life — your kids have left town, your job is in jeopardy, your house is worth nothing — until you can't think about it any more. Then don't.

There, don't you feel better?

REFERENDUM OF THE CENTURY

❖

THE BEST THING about the O.J. Simpson trial is that something finally bumped the referendum off the front page. For the last week, cries of Oui and Non were drowned out by shouts of Guilty and Not Guilty, while anglo dinner conversations in Quebec got a much-needed mid-referendum break.

Unfortunately, the holiday is over. As the "trial of the century" ends American reporters will be desperately searching for a hot new story to replace it — and don't be surprised if their heads turn north toward Quebec.

I've already been called by journalists from the U.S., France and Germany wondering what's up. Imagine the coverage if the world's press corps leaves L.A. and descends on Montreal to breathlessly cover "The referendum of the century." I can picture the scene:

"Hello America!

This is Stone Forrest, live from the streets of Montreal, a tense, divided city — though it looks deceptively calm on the surface. So far, I don't see any rioting or looting, not even any graffiti, except for a few signs that say: YES — He's Guilty!

But beneath this idyllic appearance lurks one of the longest-running and most tempestuous political trials in North American history. And we're here to bring it to you — live!

The defendant in this trial is Canada, a cold, quiet country that doesn't normally express much emotion. The prosecution is Kweebec, a hot-blooded province that accuses Canada of three centuries of abuse and humiliation.

The jury: the Kweebecois people. So welcome to "Canada on Trial!" And to introduce you to the players, let's go to our colour commentator, Ima Starr.

STARR: Thanks, Stone. Well, the separatist forces have fielded an all-star prosecution team, and it's spending millions to convince the jury to find Canada guilty. Leading the attack is Jock Parizeau, a theatrical performer who's a cross between F. Lee Bailey and Barnum and Bailey. Let's watch a clip of him in action, as he cross-examines a major defence witness.

PARIZEAU: Monsieur Chrétien, is it or is not true, that on the night of Nov. 5, 1981, you and Pierre-Elliott Trudeau stabbed Quebec in the back with several long knives, as well as a notwithstanding clause?

CHRÉTIEN: OK, OK, but let's not make an anti-federalism case out of it.

PARIZEAU: Great Scott, your Honour I demand a DNA test to see if this man is actually of Quebec origin.

FORREST: The prosecution also features Lucien Bouchard, the Johnnie Cochran of Quebec, a passionate man whose words go straight to the heart of many French jury members. Here's a clip of him in action:

BOUCHARD: My fellow Quebecers, after separation we will not really be a separate country. We will be separate but together, sovereign but united, independent but interdependent with Canada, in a kind of sovereignty-association-partnership-unity-separation!

STARR: The Canadian defence team is a solid team, though so far they've looked lacklustre. They say their client has been framed, set up by contaminated evidence and a biased prosecution. Any truth to that Stone?

FORREST: Well, statistics, studies and documents fly back and forth here in Quebec faster than bullets in Los Angeles streets. I've been polled three times myself since I got off the plane this morning.
    Early in the trial, one prosecution's expert witness, Richard Le Hir, produced 40 separate studies that all found Canada guilty of cheating Quebec. But his testimony came apart under cross-examination when the Canadian defence team found he had held back a critical study.

Here's the clip, by the Canadian leader, Jean Chrétien:

CHRÉTIEN: Your Honor, this evidence is tainted, one-sided and outrageous. We demand to see the missing evidence. Where is the bloody study?

STARR: Wow! You know, Stone, one of the most fascinating things to watch in this trial is the difference between the Canadian legal system and our own in America. This week, the PQ-led prosecution team claimed it had been violently threatened by a member of the Canadian defence team who said he wanted to "crush" the separatists in the coming referendum.

As you know, in the U.S. this would be considered a fairly tame remark, compared to the usual threats of "whipping my opponent's ass" and "kicking his butt." But in Canada, it's heavily-frowned upon to use any verb stronger than "win," "defeat" or "share in mutual victory." In fact, PQ prosecutors took out full-page newspaper ads claiming the word "crush" strayed dangerously into the area of metaphor and hyperbole — which are both illegal in Canadian politics.

FORREST: OK, now what about the jury, Stone? How are they expected to lean?

STARR: Well, most polls indicate the jury will find Canada innocent, but in an emotional case like this it's hard to be sure. A lot of people thought O.J. would be found guilty.

Most English-speaking jury members are sure to acquit Canada, but no one is sure how the French-speaking voters will break down. As the referendum verdict approaches, many wonder if the PQ prosecution will play the inflammatory language card and risk dividing the community. Or will they take the high road and risk losing the referendum with respect?

Either way, if the vote to acquit Canada gets a strong majority from the jury, an appeal seems virtually impossible. However, if the vote is very close, it could keep the case alive and lead to a retrial at the end of the century.

So we could be back for Part 2 of this "trial of the century" playing in the next century, in a post-Millennium Re-Referendum!

THE ENDUM

❖

[NOVEMBER 1995] MONTREAL, CANADA:
Well, it's nice to be back here in Canada — we almost didn't make it. The referendum night vote swung back and forth so many times I started suffering from multiple country personality disorder. In fact, I almost became a foreign correspondent without leaving home.

But how are *you* feeling? Are you suffering from post-traumatic referendum stress syndrome? Do you have referendum rash? Nationhood nightmares? Flu chez nous?

If so, you have good reason. You've just taken an exciting vacation to a panic-stricken land scarred by currency crises and passport lineups, earth-shaking referendums and resignations. And you didn't even leave home.

It was a nerve-wracking experience, but now you've got to put it behind you. It's time to return to normal life with the 10-Step Referendum Recovery Program. It's the only way to put an endum to your referendum.

1. Go cold turkey. Throw the referendum out of your life like an unwanted guest. Go through the house and get rid of all referendum literature: YES and NO pamphlets, voting lists, registration forms, even your copy of Bill 1 — the Act Respecting a Sovereign Quebec. You won't be needing it, for now.

Banish the R-word from family life. Do not read the newspaper. Do not watch news about Canada. Take a baby step toward weaning yourself from Referendum News Dependency, and rent a video tonight: *Die Hard II*.

2. Act out your feelings. Face it — you are angry and fed up, so why hide it? Take a hint from Lucien Bouchard's young children. Thursday, Bouchard said they hate the word "referendum" so much that "they spit when they pronounce it." Do the same.

3. Take life one day at a time. If you get through today, anything can happen tomorrow. Monday, Jacques Parizeau made an ugly speech that

149

left you incredibly upset. Next day — poof — he was no longer premier. Who knows what tomorrow might bring? With luck, it won't include Bernard Landry.

4. Join a referendum support group, and find a buddy to help you through bad moments. Say you wake up at 4 a.m. with a post-referendum nightmare: *You're standing in the ballot booth and you freeze up and mark the wrong ballot, and Quebec separates and Canada falls apart and IT'S ALL YOUR FAULT!*

Just call your buddy. He won't mind you waking him up — because he's having the same nightmare.

5. Face the pain: You can't leave Quebec, because no one will buy your house. Besides, running away will only make things worse, until The Problem is resolved. If anglos like you leave the city, the YES side will hold another referendum and win, and Canada will fall apart and The Problem will follow you.

You'll be living in Ottawa and suddenly it will be the capital of a former country — with 25% of Canadian MPs out of work and marauding gangs of ex-civil servants demanding your wallet.

Or you'll be out in Alberta, or B.C., and find yourself swept up in a terrifying new series of Neverendum Referendums about the question that won't go away: whether to secede from the Rest of Canada and join the U.S.

6. Reduce stress. If you're nervous or having trouble sleeping, close your eyes and try this visual relaxation trick.

Imagine the referendum is a big package.

Place the package on an imaginary canoe.

Push the canoe out into an imaginary lake.

Sink the canoe.

7. Look after your inner federalist child. During the referendum, you got in touch with something you didn't know you cared about so much — Canada. Don't be ashamed of it. Put a little maple leaf on your dashboard. Hum the national anthem at hockey games. Join the Mounties.

And thank Jacques Parizeau for helping you overcome whatever guilt you may have had about voting NO.

8. Think positively. If you voted NO, tell yourself you're still a good citizen, even though your Premier says you're not. To improve your self-esteem, say: "I'm an ethnic and proud of it."

I know some of you old-stock anglos are upset Parizeau didn't inlude you in his tirade against "money and the ethnic vote." After all, you voted NO in large numbers too — why don't you matter enough to be denounced?

In the old days, separatists called you Westmount Rhodesians, square-heads and *maudit anglais*. Now, you're not even worth a mention. Well, don't feel excluded. These days, anyone who votes NO is automatically considered ethnic.

9. Accept the things you cannot change. If you are a YES voter, remember this wasn't really a defeat. Most of us want Quebec to stay French and strong; we just see different ways of achieving it. And time will reveal whether our way can work.

Besides, only independence is forever. So let's not rush it. I know the NO side only won by 53,000 votes — but the PQ won the last provincial election by just 14,000 votes. They got a five-year mandate, so we deserve at least as much time.

10. As in all self-help courses, remember to believe in a Higher Power, because there is one in Quebec, for now.

It's called the federal government.

And now . . .

SURVIVOR LIKE ME

❖

FORGET THE PAMPERED CAST MEMBERS of the show "Survivor," who spend their time lolling around a nice desert island, surrounded by a dozen camera crews. All they have to do to survive is eat the occasional rat for ratings and play some silly games called "immunity challenges," such as throwing spears at jugs.

If you want to see a real survivor, I'm the one to watch. I've just lived through my own version of "Survivor," tested to see what modern urban man can live without — and it's been a lot tougher than a tropical island.

DAY 1: The "game" started when the renovaters arrived at our house, a topic I'd promised myself not to write about. I mean every columnist describes the same petty renovation hassles: the early morning noise, the displacement, the dust, the plaster, the rooms sealed off by plastic sheets and TOTAL UTTER CHAOS THAT TAKES OVER YOUR LIFE.

But don't sweat the small stuff. If you can't stand the heat in the kitchen, don't renovate it. Besides, the renovation isn't my real problem: it's just the backdrop to my survival game, the desert island where my other challenges take place.

DAY 4: The game started in earnest halfway through our renovation, when we made a late-night decision to abandon our house and go to the country for some calm. That's when we faced our first "immunity challenge."

We got onto the Eastern Townships Autoroute at midnight Friday, with our four-and-half-year-old son Daniel asleep in the back seat. But a half hour later, a small yellow light lit up on the instrument panel. We looked it up in our all-French car manual and it said something about "un anomalie dans les systèmes antipollution." It advised us to drive slowly and look for a dealer. Unfortunately it was 1 a.m. on a dark highway and dealers were not easy to come by. We continued driving and everything seemed fine, until we exited onto a smaller road and smelled

155

something burning — the car.

We pulled into a lot and abandoned ship around 2:30 a.m. I eventually found a pay phone and tracked down the nearest taxi, 40 km away; then we waited in the dark for an hour till the driver found us and delivered us to our country house, for a $65 tab.

We fell asleep at 6 a.m., but at least our son had slept through the whole thing and we were all safe. We had survived our second challenge — but who knew the game was only starting?

DAY 5: We had the car towed to a country garage, where the mechanic soon had that "I–hate–to–tell–you–this–Mr. Freed" look on his face. The car was only five years old with a mere 74,000 km, but we had overheated the engine so badly we had cracked the engine's head and possibly the block. I felt like a blockhead.

Next day, we got a lift back into the city with some friends, while our car got a lift in by tow truck.

DAY 8: Our car was at the garage, our house was still under construction and my office was filled with workmen. I was falling badly behind on a big deadline, so I called some friends who were leaving town and they offered me their key. I moved my laptop computer into their Westmount home, and presto — I was back in business.

I worked all morning and went out for a bite, then returned to find I was facing a new survival challenge: their door wouldn't open. Somehow a second lock had kicked in and the key was with my friends 120 km. away. I rammed the door; I rang the neighbors; I tried every window and balcony door — but I was stuck outside and my computer was inside.

I spent the afternoon in a nearby pay phone tracking down my friends, then waiting for them to track down their landlord. At 6 p.m., after six hours of prowling the street, someone showed up to let me in.

I grabbed my computer and fled home, where the noise of the renovation now seemed practically relaxing. My automobile dealer had finally called with a verdict on our car: the entire engine, radiator and electrical system had melted — the worst damage they'd seen on this model in years.

It needed a new motor, at a price that was heart-stopping. Had my car been voted off the island?

DAY 9: Next morning I had a new challenge to worry about. My fancy three-month-old computer wasn't working and the screen flashed a disturbing message: "DISC FAILURE. DO NOT OPERATE."

I told myself to stay calm. It's just a computer, I said, a computer with all your files in it — and you *write* for a living! *Stay calm.* Then I took a cab across town to my computer shop where I spent four hours watching them "defragment" my disc.

I got home around 8 p.m. and found that in the confusion of the day, I had made a new mistake: I'd lost my key chain with the keys for my house, my office, my Westmount friends' home and my car. My only mode of transport was my bike, which was fastened to our front stairs by a big lock, whose key was also on the lost chain. I would need a locksmith to cut it off, though I decided to wait a day and see if the keys turned up.

Bad decision.

DAY 10: My computer crashed again and my computer shop advised me to send it back to the manufacturer in California. I bundled up the machine, stuck it in a cab and away it went, leaving me houseless, keyless, carless, computerless and barred from by bike.

I felt like I was participating in that other TV contest show, "1900 House," where contestants live in a special house with no 20th century technology. But at least they *have* a house.

"Oh, quit whining!" I can hear some of you saying. "It's all just small stuff. Many people don't have cars or computers to break, and some don't have house keys to lose, because they have no house. So a few things went wrong — enjoy what you have."

I agree — that's exactly what I told myself. Until I went outside and discovered my bike was no longer locked to the front balcony. The lock had been cut right through, and the bike was gone, saving me the trouble of calling a locksmith.

In one week I had been stripped of all the accoutrements of modern life, in a truer test of modern survival than anything TV can serve up. I'm still telling myself not to sweat the small stuff, but the trouble is that enough small stuff starts to feel big. And I can't even win a million dollars.

Anyway, I better go. I think I may have another "immunity challenge" coming up. The phone is ringing and these days that means trouble. It could be my garage, or my computer shop, or my renovators. But more likely, someone has found my keys — and robbed my house.

Don't worry, I can take it: I'm a survivor. And this island belongs to me.

www.vehiculepress.com